ONE WAY OR ANOTHER

ONE WAY OR ANOTHER

THE STORY OF A GIRL WHO LOVED ROCK STARS

Nikki McWatters

Published by Black Inc.,
an imprint of Schwartz Media Pty Ltd
37–39 Langridge Street
Collingwood Vic 3066 Australia
email: enquiries@blackincbooks.com
http://www.blackincbooks.com

Copyright © Nikki McWatters 2012
All Rights Reserved.
No part of this publication may be reproduced, stored in a retrieval system,
or transmitted in any form by any means electronic, mechanical, photocopying, recording
or otherwise without the prior consent of the publishers.

National Library of Australia Cataloguing-in-Publication entry
McWatters, Nikki.
One way or another / Nikki McWatters.
ISBN: 9781863955560 (pbk.)
McWatters, Nikki.
Teenage girls--Queensland--Gold Coast--Biography.
Groupies--Queensland--Gold Coast--Biography.
Teenage girls--Sexual behavior--Queensland--Gold Coast.

305.2352092

Cover design by Thomas Deverall
Book design and typesetting by Peter Long

CONTENTS

Part 1
Run to Paradise
1

Part 2
Welcome to the Jungle
73

Part 3
Reckless
147

Epilogue
235
Postscript
239
Acknowledgements
241

For Ben and Toby, the best things to come out of the eighties

Part 1.

RUN TO PARADISE

1.

My first orgasm shocked my system with a welcome surprise as I writhed beneath a giant colourful stuffed rabbit named Andy Gibb. I was thirteen. Perhaps the association of extreme pleasure with rock stars began then. I had not actually been thinking of anything other than the physical sensations, but every time I watched Andy Gibb on *Countdown* after that, it brought a smile to my face. Rock and roll was the only sensible sex education I had.

Admittedly my parents, both school teachers, had sat me down with a 'birds and bees' book and given me a Catholic version of 'the talk'. I was shown infantile pictures of plants being pollinated, chickens and dogs jumping on each other's backs and finally a series of cartoon reproductive organs. The actual mating of humans was cloaked in secrecy and innuendo. The picture that accompanied the stilted text was of a couple having a cuddle under a blanket. It didn't dawn on me until some time later, when I discovered *Cosmopolitan* and *Dolly*, that penetration was part of the deal. There was no mention of pleasure and certainly not of passion. My parents had taught me, very capably, how to make babies – but rock and roll was to teach me how to have sex.

It was in 1981 in sun-drenched Surfers Paradise that, at the age of fifteen, my lustful rock and roll dreams began to manifest. I saw a bumper sticker once that declared, 'You must have one grand passion.' Mine was rock stars.

With my Flock of Seagulls hairdo, a slash of red slicing my cheekbones and a pirate shirt puffed up over black leggings, I waited at the café in Southport for my posse to arrive. A milkshake wand whirred in the background, competing with Freddie Mercury's falsetto from the radio. The bored waitress, her zippered yellow uniform stretched uncomfortably across her ample chest, gave an eye-roll of disapproval as Rhonda, Tammy and Caroline arrived like a sirocco of colour. While my hair was teased spectacularly into its lopsided shape, it was still a forgettable shade of mouse. Rhonda had gone one step further and had tips of bright red feathered through her dark hair. We all wore make-up like it was war paint. We were teenage Amazons.

Like a secret society, Rhonda, Tammy, Caroline and I would meet for milkshakes on the weekend and talk music. They were boarders at one of Queensland's most prestigious girls' colleges, or 'prisoners', as they were referred to by the day students. I was enrolled in another Catholic school nearby, but tonight they had invited me into the inner sanctum of their dormitory for an evening of fun. It was Sunday and Dad was collecting me from outside their school at nine.

After slurping down our bubbly vanilla froth, the girls and I made our way past 'Dero Park', so named for the transient drunks that littered the benches. One old fellow thrust his urine-soaked crotch at us and shouted something unintelligible but clearly pornographic. The streets of Southport were hushed and eerily empty on a Sunday. On weekdays they were filled with the chaotic bustle of suits and uniforms, squealing school buses and impatient traffic.

We passed the Gold Coast Hospital and the used-car yards and eventually reached the white picket fence surrounding the school. The historic building sat primly as an old English schoolmarm. St Hilda's. As I was not only not a boarder but not even a student there, we had to be covert. Head down, eyes averted, heart sparring with my ribcage, I was bustled into the dormitories without being identified as an alien intruder.

Inside, their three-bed room was divided by strategically placed wardrobes. Posters adorned the walls and funky bedspreads and photo boards gave the place the vibe of an adolescent cubby house. I was pickled with jealousy. It was a far cry from the Dickensian boarding schools we'd read about in English class. Spot checks and routine visits from the dorm mother occurred every hour or so, but the girls in the next room had been instructed to bang three times on the wall to warn us. I would slither under Rhonda's bed until the danger passed.

At 6.30 we switched on the television set in the corner of the room. The TV event of the year was about to hit Channel 2 – the *Countdown* Awards. Tammy cracked open a bottle of contraband Dimple Scotch and we grimaced and giggled at the horrid burning taste. When the *Countdown* intro appeared on screen with its hypnotic disco lights, we were entranced. Countdooowowowown. Each of us had adopted a favourite band. I cheered on Australian Crawl. Rhonda championed INXS, thinking Michael Hutchence the bee's knees (he was a little too pale and weedy for me). Caroline liked the rough and tumble of Cold Chisel while Tammy had her sights set on Mondo Rock. As we scoffed jelly babies and freckles and furtively swilled the Scotch, our voices crept dangerously louder. There was one close call with a dorm teacher and I banged my head hard when I scampered under Rhonda's bed with the bottle.

'Not bloody Cold Chisel again. They're awful,' Rhonda whinged as they romped home with several awards. I got up and shimmied when Australian Crawl's frontman, James Reyne, won best male artist and I entertained lusty thoughts as the band bumped out a performance of 'The Boys Light Up'. The song spoke of a flat in Surfers Paradise and I wondered if I'd ever get to see it. We stared in silence as Cold Chisel destroyed the stage during their final number and then sat around for a while, finishing the Scotch and analysing our heroes and their big night.

'Rock stars will sleep with anyone and they love schoolgirls,' Rhonda whispered.

'How do you meet one?' Tammy's wide brown eyes flickered.

'Just turn up at the backstage door looking slutty,' Rhonda grinned. 'I'm up for it.'

'I'm up for it,' I sang back, feeling the alcohol pulse through my bloodstream like a slow bluesy rhythm. Rhonda gave a devilish smirk.

'Let's make a secret club. A rock-star fan club but ... different.'

'Yeah,' I smiled and nodded. 'Like a collectors' club. We'll set targets. Rock stars. And see how close we can get to them. We'll collect them like butterflies!'

'Yeah,' Rhonda's eyes and teeth looked ghostly in the dimmed lights. 'We'll hunt 'em. Like prey. A bronze medal for seeing a rock star in person. A silver medal for talking to them. And a gold one for ...'

We all did our own version of simulating sex and laughed way too loudly.

'The Vulture Club,' Rhonda raised her empty glass to ours.

'The Vulture Club,' we clinked back.

And so the Vulture Club was born.

2.

Surfers Paradise was a tacky whore of a town. A voluptuous mass of white beaches and verdant hinterland, she had sold her soul for a few strings of sequins. The rickety fibro beach shacks could still be found cowering between the towering monstrosities that reached greedily to the sun, but they were drowning in the deepening shadows. Surfers had taken her first taste of glitter and she was addicted. Her breasts were still perky and her bloodshot eyes glistened, but an emptiness was invading her soul. She was already jaded.

While my schoolmates were bobbing beyond the breakers on salty surfboards, I was huddled in a darkened room listening to music and indulging in sordid fantasies involving entire rock bands. The anthemic sounds of the seventies had mellowed through the years into a flaccid digital drone, with only sweaty, testosterone-laced pub rock for relief. Bad skin and a cockatoo hairstyle were my uniform and I wore them with self-conscious pride. I was sitting on the ledge of life, eager to free-fall into my future.

The mirror in my suburban bedroom revealed a strangely interesting face. Pretty but in a flawed way, put together like a hasty collage. Almond-shaped green eyes that were often described as catlike. Childish, striking, but with a sinister sharpness. My breasts leapt into rooms ahead of me yet I was chicken-leg thin. The gaps in my teeth meant I smiled and spoke through tight lips, smearing my face with a permanent look of disappointment.

The only time I spoke and laughed freely was on stage, with the audience too far away to notice the mess behind my lipstick.

I had inherited my father's love of theatre. He had hung up his acting dreams and become an English teacher, nurturing a new generation of dramatists and tackling the odd amateur role at the local playhouse. A sense of safety and warmth washed over me on stage; it was a place of high visibility and invisibility, simultaneously. A hushed auditorium with all eyes trained on me, staring through the darkness up to that one spot of light – it was an addictive sensation.

From the age of ten or eleven I would ride my Malvern Star pushbike to Broadbeach at first light a couple of mornings each week. Spiral notebook tucked under my arm, biro jabbing me through my back pocket, bell-bottom jeans flapping like the clappers. Kicking off my shoes, I'd stab my way up and over the empty dunes to the beach, the soles of my feet biting into the soft sand, sounding like tiny squeals of pain.

Watching the sky change colour while noisy seagulls scattered like silver confetti, I wrote poetry. It felt like Shakespeare in my heart but when I read my words back they were forced and awkward; I was trying on emotions that didn't quite fit. My dreams on that beach were of fame and fortune. An Oscar. A rock-star lover. Perfect teeth. I filled pages and pages with manic doodles until the sun warmed the morning and the grey of the ocean began to stir itself into a sparkle of lapis lazuli. Then a quick pedal home through the morning traffic crush, a piece of burnt toast topped with peanut paste and a cup of Milo, and I'd pack my port and get dressed for another day of school.

By 1981, however, my morning routine had begun to change. It was no longer so cool to ride a Malvern Star and the beach was becoming crowded with early joggers, tourists washing away hangovers and southern retirees walking overweight Labradors. High-rises popped up like warts along the esplanade and a slick of coconut oil stained the water's edge. At fifteen I found that I preferred to be in my warm, musky bed, thinking about sex, wondering what it might be like, creating erotic poetry in my head.

My parents had a very definite idea of what path my life should take: I was to be a Catholic schoolteacher, married to some well-heeled professional. My protestations that I wanted to be a famous actress were met with comments such as 'That's not real life' and 'You don't have Hollywood teeth.' I felt like a pressure cooker of repressed potential. To be 'normal' or 'sensible' was intolerable. I wanted to be loud, unpredictable, sassy and spontaneous. I wanted to shine like a beacon, not sit quietly under a lampshade.

At school, I played the game and appeared to bow to the will of the nuns, who taught us that boys were evil and sex was a terrible ordeal women had to endure in order to populate the planet. The Sisters of Mercy taught us that Lucifer himself had designed condoms and that so much as to touch one would ensure eternal damnation.

I didn't have the tools or the confidence to take on the nuns or my parents to their faces. They were like huge pillars of righteousness throwing giant shadows across my spotlight. But deep inside me, a burlesque showgirl was tapping her heels, waiting for her chance to do some shocking high-kicks. I would bide my time and look for my opportunity to escape.

My parents insisted that I play the church organ at St Vincent's every Sunday. The wailing of the talcum-powdered biddies and the discordant din of my pedalling turned me off Christianity for life. Some Sundays I had to do a Bible reading from the pulpit as well. Then there was the rote confessional and repetitive, meaningless penance. I usually lied about my sins to the priest, just made them up, until eventually I had to say, 'Bless me, Father, for I have sinned. It has been two weeks since my last confession. These are my sins. I have lied about all previous sins.' Ten Hail Marys or so and the slate was wiped clean.

Lying seemed preferable to confessing my real sins, most of which were only thoughts about sin, but those of course still counted. 'These are my sins. I rub myself up against a giant rabbit called Andy Gibb for pleasure. I dream of shallow fame and fabulous wealth and I have a list in my underwear drawer of all the rock stars I would like to bed.' That might have resulted in a stricter penance.

My parents' academic expectations were not reflected in my term reports, which unanimously observed that I was a dreamer. In 1981 my marks in every subject except drama fell somewhere in the alphabet below the letter D. Diverting my mid-year report card from the mailbox to my bedroom, I forged my mother's signature and returned it to the school as required. Of course the head nun did not believe my parents could be so blasé and telephoned my mother. Mum was inconsolable and I feared she might disown me.

'You've brought such shame upon the family. I don't think I can ever hold my head up in public again. This reflects upon your father and me!'

My punishment was a solid period of grounding and a Cinderella-esque list of household chores, from scrubbing mouldy shower recesses to collecting ten large buckets of leaves from the garden. I suffered my sentence in characteristic sullenness and came out the other end of it full of repressed resentment and not an iota of remorse.

As I toiled, daydreams of fame and fortune brewed. A shrink might have diagnosed me as a schizoid narcissist during adolescence, but let's just say I had a vivid imagination. Scrubbing the bathroom tiles with an old toothbrush, I drafted my Academy

Award 'thank-you' speech, a scathing attack on all the bastards who had not believed in me or my teeth. I imagined grinning with a mouthful of porcelain chompers, my bosoms bursting boldly from a red sequinned number. There are those who act purely for the love of the art. I was not one of them. I craved global adoration and enormous amounts of filthy lucre. I wanted Rod Stewart on my arm, crooning his latest love song in my ear.

In the evening my penance continued with babysitting duties, giving my parents a night off at the cinema.

'What did you see?' I asked when they returned.

'*Phar Lap*,' Mum responded dreamily. 'It was wonderful. The girl in it was so beautiful. She had such lovely teeth.'

I went to bed with a scowl and read about the actress in *Dolly* the next day. Gia Carides. And yes, she did have lovely teeth!

At night I dreamed of losing my virginity to a rock star. Sting was a possibility. James Reyne was appealingly tanned. Rick Springfield was pretty. David Lee Roth might make me laugh and Michael Hutchence looked like he knew a few moves. But Rod was always top of the list. I had loved him since I was twelve. To my teenage mind, there was nothing sexier than a leather-trousered rock star. Schoolboys were gangly and spotty and stupid. I wanted a real man, not an embryonic one.

Nevertheless, schoolboys would have to do in the meantime. For real flesh and blood boyfriends, I looked to the theatre. The annual inter-school drama festival, organised by my father, was the pinnacle of my social calendar. Backstage I found my first fake kisses and first false declarations of desire. My first crush on a real boy ended tragically when he hanged himself from a rafter in a school theatre. I had barely spoken to Chris but we had all admired him from a distance. Huddles of schoolgirls cried with melodramatic anguish. Suddenly he had been everyone's best friend. The bell tolled for us all.

Teachers avoided any discussion of the subject, fearing a rash of copycat behaviour. Chris had been an exemplary student – gifted at music, academics and acting. Talk was that he had had his heart set on being a Shakespearean actor and was gutted when a teacher told him to forget the dream. Chris was of Chinese heritage and it was pointed out to him that there were no Chinese characters in Shakespeare's plays. It might work in the school theatre, he'd been counselled, but not on the world stage. If this was his dramatic answer to such narrow-mindedness, I thought, there was something poetic and noble about the act. I made Chris my patron saint of schoolboys for a while.

My tight-knit group of girlfriends from my Catholic college, Star of the Sea, had little time for the lads from our brother school, Aquinas. We preferred a better cut of meat: the boys from The Southport School. There were four girls and four boys in our little tribe and over the course of year eleven we paired off with each other in turn. I held hands with Alan, went boating with Richard and then doe-see-doed into Sean's arms in time for his school formal. We never really dated in the traditional sense. No moonlit dinners or romantic strolls on the beach. Instead we groped and fondled with naïve and apprehensive hands in borrowed bedrooms and the back seats of cars. Despite my interest, I never managed to get past about second base.

By the end of year eleven my final marks were dismal and the principal, Sister Annette, dropped a bombshell: I lacked the 'emotional maturity' to move into year twelve and would have to repeat. Horrified, my parents decided I should transfer to the rough-as-guts public school where my father taught. It was pointless to argue: the gavel had struck the bench and my sentence was not open to appeal. Besides, I had bigger issues on my mind. As I contemplated the long summer holidays and swapped torrid fantasies with the Vultures, my lust throbbed along like a thumping bass section. It was time to turn my rock and roll daydreams into reality.

3.

In early January of 1982, with stars in my eyes and butterflies in my knickers, I attended my very first rock gig. Australian Crawl performed at Bombay Rock, a gritty nightclub on the darker edge of Surfers, down the river end of Cavill Avenue. Posters of touring bands plastered the concrete walls and a narrow ramp lead to the front entrance. When a big name came to town, the queue of punters could wind all the way up to the Pacific Highway, inching its way towards the bouncers on the door.

Inside, the smell of beer and sweat was stale but sweet. Lights beckoned from the two bars, one upstairs, one down, glasses and bottles glistening behind the busy staff. Up against the stage, the dance pit was thick with tanned young people stomping and pogo-dancing to the tracks spilling from the DJ deck. Strategically placed fake pot-plants provided receptacles for their cigarette butts and vomit. The whole place reeked of a summer hangover, the stench of sea-salt and coconut oil spilling from day into night. Paradise by strobe light.

We had chosen a busy night, hot and humid with the smell of a storm in the air. The young surf-rockers from Mornington Peninsula belted out unintelligible lyrics to a hypnotic beat while I pressed against the stage, a tidal wave of kids pushed up behind me. The band gyrated and sweated and the sound possessed my body, writhing through my veins like an erotic python.

After worshipping my idols from the floor I abandoned my friends with tunnel-visioned determination. I would take my virginity backstage and thrust it at whichever musician wanted it. They had played me into a frenzy and I figured one of them could damn well put that fire out.

I wore a tight pair of stonewashed jeans and a pink and grey sloppy joe. My feet were interred in unimpressive Kmart sandshoes. My mother still supervised my wardrobe and I couldn't see her going for the brazenly slutty look of the groupie uniform. The diehard rock lobsters lined up at the backstage door looked more the part, tottering on white high heels and squeezed into impossibly tiny white miniskirts. Their fringed leather minijackets framed leathery brown cleavages and each sun-bleached face wore an entire make-up department. In truth, I had never given much thought to what a real groupie looked like. My confidence took a nosedive as I lined up with the others, all of us hoping for a chance to rub shoulders or more with the band.

At the front of the queue I spotted Lyn Barron, a *Playboy* centrefold and local celebrity. I recognised her from her frequent appearances as a page-three girl in the *Gold Coast Sun*. Sensing that my chance to find true love with a sweaty musical god was slipping away, I figured I might as well get at least a brush with celebrity and force a B-grade Playboy Bunny to say hello to me. Shuffling my way forward, I boldly introduced myself.

Lyn blinked and looked confused, but she was gracious and asked who I was going backstage to see. Just then the door burst open and a stocky roadie scanned the perfumed selection before him. He nodded to Lyn and licked his lips. Lyn smiled her beautiful smile, put her arm around my shoulder and said, 'She's with me.' In a flash we were ushered into the hallowed hallway leading to the Holy Grail – the Green Room.

My stomach was in knots and I needed to pee badly. The stark fluorescent walls and concrete echo seemed surreal. Lyn asked my name and in a blur of faces introduced me to the band, as well as a few vaguely familiar beautiful people. I stood gulping like a goldfish, feeling suddenly ridiculous. Dressed more like a teenage boy than a glamorous bird of paradise, I accepted a glass of champagne and knocked it back fast. I had walked into one of my own fantasies.

Soon I was attempting to make small talk with James Reyne. He was so good-looking and smelled so unmistakeably *male*, I was tongue-tied. Brad Robinson, lead guitarist, introduced himself. No-one seemed to notice that I didn't belong. In fact my strangely casual attire was so different from the norm that it seemed to attract more attention than the standard groupie cleavage.

Surprise at how easily I had invaded the party threatened to overwhelm me, but I pushed it aside and embraced the evening. More champagne. More flirtations. A few canapés. My plan had been to stay at my friend Fiona's house after the gig, but I had warned her that if I disappeared backstage she should leave without me and tell her parents I had decided to go home. My God, I couldn't wait to gloat to the other Vultures.

Suddenly it was announced that the party was travelling back to the Golden Gate, a luxury high-rise two blocks north where the band was staying. I ended up in a car driven by Guy McDonough, guitarist and songwriter, a little ferrety fellow with a nice voice. Within minutes he had lightly rear-ended another car in the convoy, to everyone's amusement. As we sped through the glittery dazzle of Surfers Paradise, the gaudy neon signs blinking seductively, I shut my eyes and opened them again in disbelief.

Back at the band's apartment, the atmosphere was charged with a tense eroticism. James Reyne lay on a bed and held court while people lazed about on the floor. It became clear that Lyn was his prize for the evening. They were mischievously familiar and it seemed she was his Gold Coast girl of the moment. The girl-in-every-port cliché appeared to be the rule for these young rock stars. James was cocky but in a self-deprecating way and I warmed to him. He seemed somehow detached from his fame, perhaps even a little embarrassed by it – although the perks obviously entertained him.

All of the guys in the band seemed to be attached to attractive blondes – except one. He was my only shot. He seemed a little shy and self-conscious, mirroring my own uncertainty. Having chosen my target, I went to work. We made eye contact across the room and I sent out loaded vibes. A wry smile tugged at his mouth and I knew he could read my thoughts. It didn't take much psychic ability. Our tennis match of eye play continued until finally he sauntered over to where I sat on the couch. I had not practised a seduction routine and yet it slid along perfectly, like a beautifully choreographed dance.

'Hi. You look lonely.' (Let's have sex.)

'I don't really know anyone.' (Fine. You'll do.)

'Want to come down to my room?' (Right now?)

'Sure.' (Sure.)

He was handsome, I thought as I studied his profile. So much more mature than my schoolboy mates. A man. A real man. He held my hand in the elevator. A big warm hand. It was about then that my nerves began to jingle-jangle. Tiny electrical currents were firing about my body and my face felt flushed. I felt out of place, like a girl masquerading as a woman. At fifteen years and eleven months, I was just shy of being 'legal'. My designated Initiator didn't seem to notice or mind and I wasn't going to volunteer my date of birth. If he'd asked, I'd have said I was seventeen. Seventeen was an acceptable age. But he didn't ask. He didn't say very much at all. He did ask me what I did for a living and I told him I was an actress. He liked actresses, he replied.

Little did he know I was right in the middle of an award-winning performance and he was the prize.

The Initiator's room was basic but comfortable. I poured a lemonade while he rang his full-time woman in Melbourne. Not wanting to alert the unsuspecting woman to the fact that an under-aged tomboy was about to be de-virginised, I was careful not to make much noise.

It was all very businesslike. I hadn't chosen him because of some pulsing chemical attraction but because he had a 'vacancy' sign in his eyes. He was attractive but not really my type. Rod Stewart was my type. But he *was* a rock star and he'd been on *Countdown*. It was the sexual equivalent of an arranged marriage. He met certain vital criteria and now he was my designated guide.

As he led me to the bedroom, I tiptoed behind him on jellyfish legs.

'Light on or off?' he asked.

'Off,' came my speedy response. I didn't want him to see the alarm on my face.

I sat on the bed, rigid and numb. My heart was tap-dancing in my chest and my hands were shaking, so I sat on them. The Initiator stripped down to nothing, like it was all in a day's work. The light from the hallway spilled across the carpet and formed a halo around his nakedness. 'It' seemed impossibly large and I began to have second thoughts. I'd assumed it would be about the size of a finger, but this thing was standing up like a ridiculous new limb. The Boys Light Up and how!

The Initiator sat beside me and his hands feathered through my hair as he leaned forward to kiss me. His tongue and lips felt bigger and bolder than the few I'd previously sampled. I lay down, but when his warm hands slipped my jeans over my hips I had a moment of panic. It didn't last long. I'd felt stage fright many times before and knew it would only help my performance.

Embarrassment soon gave way to urgency as he tinkled his fingers over my ivory flesh, doing things I'd only ever done to myself.

I let my own hands explore his hard edges and strong muscles and felt like an uneasy adventurer, delving into uncharted territory. With a deft movement he knelt between my thighs and I took a deep breath, shut my eyes tightly and waited.

It didn't hurt. I opened my eyes in surprise. I'd been braced for pain but it was more of a friendly invasion. I'd done a fair bit of horse-riding as a young girl and suspect that might have played some part ... or perhaps God had built me without a hymen. What worried me most was whether I was supposed to move beneath him or just lie there. I rocked with him a little in case that was the done thing. It all seemed a bit mechanical. There was no earth-shattering explosion of stars, just a fuzzy feeling of warmth and connection. The whole thing was over in a few minutes.

'Was that good for you, then?' he whispered into my ear.

'Ahh ... yep. Fine.'

The poor fellow had no idea he'd just sponsored my promotion into adulthood.

The Initiator asked me if I wanted to have a shower with him, but I got dressed, thanked him for the sex and returned to the party. No-one noticed that I had taken that great leap for womankind except perhaps Lyn, who gave me a conspiratorial smile.

It was something of an anticlimax, I thought, as I walked home in the early hours of the morning. The cars sped down the highway. The neon lights winked at me. A police car screamed by, its red lights pirouetting like a fiery ballerina. Did I feel different? Yes. I felt a little bit more worldly. I felt like the door to a secret chamber had been opened to me. Had I found what I expected? Not really. I'd expected a rock star to be something special. Something magical and larger than life. But he'd just been flesh and blood. Warm skin. Nice lips. Polite but insipid.

I'd made it through the wilderness but to be honest, Andy Gibb was better!

4.

My debut as a bona fide groupie launched me into uber-popularity amongst the St Hilda harlots. I had fired the pistol and the race was on. The other girls were disadvantaged by their status as boarders but began plotting rock and roll adventures for the school holidays. By the end of the Easter break Rhonda was leading the pack, the blood of hapless rock stars dribbling down her gorgeous chin.

Rhonda spent every second weekend with her family in Brisbane, which greatly expanded her selection of venues. Before long she was mixing with INXS and gleefully regaling us with juicy stories. Although they were perched on the brink of international glory, at this stage the young band was still playing the university circuit.

The Vulture Club developed a manifesto. Groupies had to be focused and unemotional. We were hunters and collectors. Falling in love was not an option. It was an edgy hobby, not a way to find a long-term boyfriend. Truth be told, a rock star in real life would make a hopeless partner. Far better to be a rock and roll mistress than a rock and roll missus. Musicians were junk food, not a proper nutritious meal. Good and bad for you at the same time, like a plate of greasy chips and a bottle of red, red wine.

These young men became our imaginary friends. We circled saucy bits in the pages of *Cleo* and *Cosmopolitan*, having graduated from *Dolly*, which was far too juvenile. I learned in black and white about fellatio and cunnilingus and realised there were more ways than one to skin a rock star. Some of the things we read about were hard to imagine. But we tried very, very hard.

Rhonda's modus operandi was slightly different from mine. She targeted the road crew. 'No-one loves a roadie, but oh how a roadie can love' was her motto. It was an indirect route that often paid off.

Tammy was spunky and hilarious but she was more of a spectator. She loved the stories and the bands but as far as I know she kept her legs firmly crossed, most of the time.

Caroline was our moral compass, always keeping us from going too far and worrying about the potential dangers of our sordid pastime. She was a warm and funny girl with a smile that could melt an iceberg.

My parents were old-school and much stricter than others. I had a curfew of ten o'clock on weekends and my father insisted on dropping me off and collecting me from wherever I was going. As most headline acts didn't start until after ten, I had to think laterally if I wanted to get to rock gigs. My parents were tucked safely into bed by nine every night. My bedroom had a window. It didn't take long for me to see some wonderful possibilities.

5.

Australian Crawl were back in town. On a cool Thursday night in August, I pushed my luck and dressed in a more enticing outfit, although I was still favouring the gothic tomboy look. I carefully and ever so quietly removed the flyscreen from my window and crawled out, crept down the garden path and stole stealthily through the night, over the three bridges of Monaco Street and up the well-lit highway to Bombay Rock.

Walking through the dark felt dangerously exciting. I pushed away all thoughts of the infamous 'hitchhiker killer', who had murdered a string of girls on the Gold Coast a few years earlier. I had even attended the funeral of one victim, who had been a student at my primary school. The serial killer was still at large but I told myself firmly that I was walking, not hitchhiking.

At Bombay Rock I recognised a blonde bimbo from the previous party and made her my best friend for the evening. There was safety and a measure of success in numbers. Already a little tipsy herself, Kirsty bought me a vodka and orange and filled me in on her impressive list of achievements. The vulture culture was all about competition. She claimed to have bedded Rod Stewart's drummer, which left me speechless. To be so close!

'Ooh and Rod's sooo charming and funny,' she smiled, rubbing in the salt.

Since my opening act at the Golden Gate, opportunities had been slim. Rhonda was streaking ahead of me and I needed a win with a real musician to stay in the game. I was ravenous and desperate.

Eventually a roadie appeared at the backstage door – but this time he was carrying a list. My curly blonde friend was on the list. I was not. Of course I wasn't. I don't think I'd even bothered to introduce myself officially to the Initiator. There was no sign of Lyn Barron and I was left at the door, lost and humiliated.

I wandered out into the cool night and moped about, unsure what to do next. Fronting up to the Golden Gate might have worked, but what if the band was staying somewhere else this time? Downhearted but still determined, I walked aimlessly around to the back entrance of the four-storey building.

Suddenly somebody tugged at my sleeve. I turned to see a bearded fellow – a lumbering, hairy giant.

'You trying to get backstage?' he asked shadily.

I sized him up. Unkempt and with a slightly manic look in his eyes, he could have been a homeless person. Late twenties, about six foot two, possibly a little mad.

'I know a way in. You go up here.' He pointed up a concrete wall to an unfinished window on the third floor. Bombay Rock had been constructed some years earlier but the developers had not yet opened the top two storeys. It was a dark monolith, a largely windowless mass above the well-lit lower levels.

My desperation overshadowed my apprehension, so I smiled and urged him to show me the way. I followed him down a narrow alleyway to a drainpipe and we politely introduced ourselves before scaling the wall. He was Mick. He went first and his bulk was surprisingly agile. He reached back down to help me and I clambered after him like a little monkey. His hand was firm and he seemed to know exactly where he was going.

After landing on the cold cement floor of what appeared to be a concrete bunker, I took a moment to catch my breath. The huge, cavernous space was dimly lit with dusty light globes, abuzz with hyperactive moths.

'We follow it round to the staircase and down a flight of stairs and the doors lead straight backstage. No-one on the door. We can just wander in and join the party. I do it all the time,' he grinned confidently. Dusting myself off, I followed him across the grey expanse. Music thumped below, reverberating up my spinal column. A bad smell hung in the air like the aftertaste of dead rat.

As we rounded a concrete pillar and the stairs came into view, Mick turned suddenly and violently grabbed my wrist. It hurt. My Mickey Mouse watch snapped and clattered to the floor. His eyes burned and his sharp teeth hissed from behind his bristly beard. Panicked, I struggled and made some terrified noises. Mick just laughed.

'Don't bother screaming. No-one can hear you up here.'

He was right. Not only would no-one hear me scream, but this unused corner of the world might not be visited by another human for years. My parents would assume I'd been kidnapped from my bedroom. No-one would know where to look. I was as good as dead. The situation hit me with such force I could picture the headlines.

'Skeletal remains found in Bombay Rock may be teenager missing since 1982.' A strobe of blue lights exploded in my brain, threatening to shut it down. A stealthy numbness invaded my body.

Managing somehow to wrench my hand free, feeling the bruises seeping across my wrist, I stumbled to the staircase. Mick followed fast. At the bottom of the stairwell were two huge metal doors, firmly locked from the other side. Panting and frantic, I was cornered. Mick lurched down the stairs and grabbed me, forcing me to the ground. He pushed himself between my legs and his rancid breath came in hot bursts against my face.

I don't know where my inspiration came from in the next few moments, but my stupidity at getting myself into the situation was matched only by the brilliance of my self-rescue.

'What are you doing, Mick?' I asked with Oscar-worthy confusion. 'I thought we had something nice going on between us. Don't wreck it now.' I batted my eyelashes and gave him the smile of an innocent.

'What? Whaddya say?' He paused and pulled back to look at me.

'I really like you. Let's do this properly. I don't want to do it here. Let's go to the beach, hey?' I gave him a coy but knowing look. 'It's my first time and I want it to be special.'

He was biting his bottom lip.

'Are you for real?'

'I really like you. I thought you liked me too. I'll shout you a coffee and we can have a really nice time on the sand. I like you.'

He sat back on his haunches and looked at me. All the acting classes I had ever done came down to this moment. I smiled, my lips twitching in time with my hammering heartbeat. Finally he smiled back. I wasn't sure if it was a real smile or a murderous leer.

'Cool. Hey, I'm really sorry about your watch.' He pulled me to my feet.

Touching my hair, he spoke gently.

'Hey, you're pretty. So, you'll really let me do it to you on the beach?'

'Sure, Mick,' I lied. 'Come on, let's get out of here.'

We walked up the stairs and he held my hand. Picking up my watch, he tried to fix it but shrugged his shoulders and gave it back to me sheepishly.

'Sorry.'

We clambered back out the window and down to the rear driveway. As we rounded the corner, I bluffed.

'Hey, Mick,' I said as casually as possible. 'I've just got to let my mates know that I won't be going home with them.'

He stopped and frowned, not sure whether to buy my line. My pulse threatened to deafen me.

'Fine,' he agreed reluctantly. 'I'll come too.'

The doorman had disappeared for the evening and just a few stragglers remained, watching the roadies packing up the gear. I had no idea what I was going to do until suddenly Brad Robinson, the guitarist, strode across the room. I hurried over to him, hopeful that he might remember me. A glimmer of recognition flickered across his handsome face.

'That guy over there just tried to rape and kill me,' I blurted, bursting into tears.

As soon as Brad looked across at Mick, the man realised he'd been double-crossed and fled. Brad put his arm around me and shepherded me backstage, offering me a much-needed drink. I refused his offer to call the police. I was sixteen and my parents would have been informed. I didn't see that as an option at all. Traumatised, I was in no mood to party and Brad arranged for a pretty roadie to take me home. I got him to drop me one block away and I padded home through the dew-damp grass. Crawling back into the safety of my bedroom and carefully replacing the screen, I fell into bed and prayed to the God I didn't believe in, thanking him for my life.

My parents wondered at my listlessness during breakfast.

'Bad dreams,' I muttered.

No word of a lie. Perhaps I had met the hitchhiker murderer after all.

6.

While the Vultures continued our predatory antics, my transfer downmarket to Southport State High brought me a new circle of friends. Catholic school had been a world apart – heaven crossed with a concentration camp – and state school was a shock to the system. This place was more like a musky, dank jungle, earthy and untamed.

Girls at my new school had pierced noses and dyed hair and there were spotty boys everywhere, their voices crackling like pond frogs. It was common enough to stumble upon a couple making out in the locker rooms. Empty crisp packets and crushed cans of cola littered the playground. Pale tendrils of smoke rose from the barred windows of the lavatory blocks like papal heralds. Teachers swore and the school uniform came in hundreds of acceptable variations. I never once pined for the convent school. I did not miss my green beret or the soapy smell of the nuns. I certainly didn't miss their uncanny alertness to teenage sexuality, any hint of which would be promptly stomped on by sensible shoes.

Having my father at school was not as awkward as I had feared. It was a big place and he didn't teach me. I soon found my niche in the theatre set, a talented but troubled troupe of loud, hormonal time bombs. I felt right at home.

We were new-wave romantics and we avoided the playground, preferring to wallow like tortured artists in the school auditorium. We wrote plays and songs and poetry. There was

Samantha, a beautiful girl with long, tangled blonde hair, dangerous blue eyes and a baby-doll air that worked beautifully with the boys. Sam's father lived far away on a hippy commune, which fascinated me. Then there was Jeanette, quiet but with a devil-may-care attitude and a laugh that sounded like the scratch of a needle across a record. Paul and Berzerko were graceful, hair-tossing boys with surly pouts, deeply handsome, dark and glowering, passionate about the theatre and both with beautiful singing voices. They had an odd love–hate relationship, alternating between flirting with one another and beating each other up.

It was a time of social awakening and the more daring boys pushed gender boundaries, taking their cues from Boy George, Freddie Mercury and Elton John. Frankie was going to Hollywood, Soft Cell sang of Tainted Love and it seemed the whole world was suddenly rainbow-coloured. But in the schoolyard, cruelty and ridicule were still thrown like rotten tomatoes at those brave kids who dared to explore.

'Jeanette's in love with you,' Sam announced to me one morning.

I was intrigued. I'd briefly had an innocent crush on Joan Jett, but after giving it some thought had decided I wanted to *be* her rather than have a romantic liaison with her. Jeanette was androgynously beautiful. Her short dark hair fell in a tumble across one eye and she had cheekbones you could ski down. Coffee-brown eyes, olive skin and athletic lines. I felt no great surge of passion but a tender curiosity.

Not long after, we danced together at a school disco, brushing together occasionally like swaying branches. A current of forbidden electricity surged between us and we stepped outside and looked awkwardly at one another. A cool night breeze messed with our carefully coiffed hair. Jeanette kissed away my apprehension with her soft girl lips and I responded. Her skin was warm and she smelled like jasmine.

The kiss lingered in my mind as I lay awake in bed that night. It had been nice. It had been titillating. But I realised there was an invisible barrier around me, a heavy, clunky structure built on Catholic paranoia. In my head I knew I had done nothing wrong. But my terror of where that path might lead and the consequent wrath I might encounter crippled me. I did not know how to fight against such a formidable enemy. My culture. My parents' religion. Society. Narrow-mindedness.

I broke Jeanette's heart and the warmth between us cooled. Jeanette and Sam fell in love for a bit after that. A green flicker of envy teased me but I shooed it away. I was jealous but proud of the young people around me who dared to stand up to intolerance.

Having failed year eleven so abysmally the first time, I was determined to lift my grades. Once or twice a week I went dutifully with Dad to the staff-room after school, escaping the distraction of my two youngest siblings to study.

At home there was tension between my parents. For some time there had been a Siberian chill but now the unspoken hostility was mounting. I loved them both, as much as a teenager could, but saw that they were as ill matched as Felix and Oscar from *The Odd Couple*, only not as funny. I wondered when they'd stopped being happy together. Had they ever been happy? There were no fights, no raging finger pointing – just a taut silence and the heavy condensation of disappointment.

At least my improving grades gave them something to be glad about. Senior year brought with it a mountain of schoolwork, but with an arrogant lack of industry I managed to produce pleasing results. The rest of the Vulture Club had graduated a year ahead of me and were soon carried away by the tertiary merry-go-round. Rhonda was studying optometry in Brisbane, Tammy was doing an acting course in Armidale and Caroline had fallen off the radar. Jealous of their adult freedoms, I threw my energies into the pub-rock scene and a spate of reckless promiscuity. Burning a lusty trail, I crossed paths with the Angels, Cold Chisel, Cheap Trick, Midnight Oil and, much to Rhonda's consternation, INXS. And I retained a very soft spot for Australian Crawl, whom I could always count on for hydration in a dry spell.

Meanwhile, I began to turn my mind to life after school. I had decided to audition for NIDA, the best acting school in the country. The auditions weren't until October but I spent months preparing. Mum and Dad were careful to point out that my chances were extremely slim, but I was confident I had what it took. I spent a long time choosing my audition pieces and immersed myself in Shakespeare, finally settling on a speech by Lady Macbeth and another by Puck, the frisky sprite from *A Midsummer Night's Dream*. I would sit in my bedroom for hours, working myself into a Lady Macbeth fury and then scampering about the shag-pile carpet like a forest sprite. I'd pose in front of the mirror and try on facial expressions like a series of masks. Ferocious. Awestruck. Cheeky. Deranged.

The theatre scene on the Gold Coast was vibrant and there was no shortage of outlets for my passion for drama. I fell in with the aspiring showbiz crowd and found myself one night at one of their glamorous parties, high up in a penthouse belonging to somebody's mother. It was my first real taste of expensive living and it tasted good.

Our host was the archetypal Mr Gold Coast, only a few years older than I was but reportedly already a self-made millionaire.

He had a teenage bikini model on his arm and surrounded himself with a cast of tawdry peacocks. He worked the room like a celebrity and then sat his golden personality down beside me, holding my hand as he talked. His eyes prickled my skin. I felt strangely hypnotised.

'And what's your story?' he asked.

Having had a few French champagnes, I decided to be direct. Whether I wanted to shock, impress or both, I can't be sure.

'I'm a schoolgirl who collects rock stars,' I laughed.

'Wonderful. That's lovely.' He patted my knee.

'Really?' I was taken aback. 'Most people would be appalled.'

'Not at all.' He shrugged. 'It's natural. Innocence doesn't last forever. Might as well take it while it lasts ...' He glanced around.

'Go on,' I encouraged.

'Well, take the Gold Coast. It was originally like an innocent young girl. Unspoilt. Virginal.' I smiled at his analogy and saw where it was going. 'But the developers took what they wanted and if it wasn't this stretch of beach it would have been another. It's evolution, progress. Now it's a free-for-all and everyone's happy.' He laughed.

'So, you're calling the Gold Coast ... a tacky slut?'

'Tacky? My word. But not a slut. Just attractive and available. She was lying there begging for it with all those beaches and tangled mangroves. She's been, shall we say, glamorised.'

He winked at me and drifted off.

At four in the morning, swilling the dregs of my warm champagne and surveying the shabby oysters, I took a mental snapshot of this two-storey penthouse with its pool, its antiques and its twinkling view and vowed to settle for nothing less. No brick veneer in the suburbs, 2.3 children and Labrador for me. I wanted it all. I wanted to go everywhere, see everything and meet everybody. Fame and fortune might be mirages, I knew – but I wanted to worship at the shrine of opulence.

As final exams approached, there was a mountain of schoolwork to get through. My parents vetoed most social invitations and I made the illicit trek to Bombay Rock less and less. But one balmy Friday night, after an Australian Crawl gig, I found myself on the rooftop of a beachfront highrise with Guy McDonough, the guitarist who had pranged the car the night of my initiation. We leaned over the rails and breathed deeply of the salty air. To the sound of crashing breakers we chatted loosely about the gig, the weather and current affairs. He had always struck me as arrogantly aloof, but tonight he seemed vulnerable and tragic.

'What do you do, then?' he asked, only half interested in my answer.

'I'm still at school.' I felt compelled to tell this man the truth.

He raised an eyebrow and whistled.

'High school, I hope.' He grinned. 'You should be at home doing your homework.'

I laughed and we sat down on the concrete, our backs resting on the wall. He told me about his school days and the frustrations of life on the road, working day in and day out with a group of fellows he didn't always get along with. His brother played drums and it sounded like they were close. I complained about my parents and their strict discipline, explaining how I crawled out my window to party in Surfers. He frowned at me.

'You're lucky your parents care about you. It's a bit of a worry, you wandering about the streets at your age. Someone will take advantage of you.'

'That's what I'm hoping for. It's worked so far.'

Was I flirting with him? I wasn't sure.

'You're a very naughty girl.' He slapped my leg and shut his eyes.

And then we talked about music. He loved song writing and told me it was his lifeboat in a sea of sharks. I had a music assignment due in a week and told him about it.

'I'm a bit ragged tonight,' he drawled. 'Wanna catch up for a coffee tomorrow?'

'Sure.' It was Friday night and I could steal away from home for an hour or so on a Saturday. I gave him my number and began the long walk home. It kept me fit and lean.

The next day my parents were off to visit my maternal grandparents in Toowoomba, a red and dusty town nearly three hours away. I begged off, citing a huge homework load. Guy rang just after they left.

'Do you want to pop round to my place and I'll make you a coffee?' I offered. 'I can play you what I've got on the piano and you can tell me if it's shit or not.'

Guy paused. I could tell he wasn't sure what I was talking about.

'Ahhh ... sure. Just quickly, and just for a coffee.'

We spent an hour tinkling at the piano and he brought my old nylon-stringed guitar to life, playing it like it had never been played before.

'You're not half bad,' he nodded as I played him my work in progress. He gave me some pointers and then sang me a new song he was working on. After an hour, he stood up and stretched.

'I gotta go,' he said. 'Can't hang around here all day. You're a schoolgirl. What would people say?' He laughed and slapped me playfully on the back as I walked him to the door.

'Catch you later. Thanks for the tips.'

'You behave,' he called as he bounded down the path.

'Never!'

I smiled and went back inside and practised my new and improved composition all day.

Despite their open-mindedness, my state-school buddies knew only the barest details of my backstage antics. While rock stars were expected to be wanton sex beasts, their partners were labelled sluts. Well aware of this double standard, I held my cards close to my chest away from the safety of the Vulture Club. It made no sense to me that men were allowed to explore their sexuality but women weren't. Weren't we sides of the same coin? Sex made me feel powerful and free and beautiful – something I lacked in my day job as a voiceless, uniformed student. I never saw the groupie set as sluts. We were rock and roll tourists, collecting souvenirs.

One night I stood at my bedroom window, watching the flat sheets of rain pour into our pool, droplets bouncing like bullets from the surface. I couldn't even see the fence or the hibiscus trees by the gate. The sound of the sudden storm was like an air-raid and my plans to throw myself at the frontman of the Radiators were drowning before my eyes. I'd been to a few of their gigs and found him strangely fascinating – odd, definitely, but also bizarrely attractive. Hawklike but sexy in a rough sort of way. I closed my curtains and pulled out some tissues to wipe the make-up from my face. No adventure that night. I was imprisoned by the weather.

My chin was sporting a constellation of spots, only half-hidden by a slash of foundation. There were dark rims, like hubcaps, under my eyes. I looked tired. The rain pelted down outside and I wondered if the Gold Coast might flood like it did in 1974. That had been kind of exciting, being rescued by boat from a neighbour's balcony. Perhaps I'd get out of school for a week or two.

But the rain eased by Friday and Rhonda came to stay for the weekend. We spent Saturday afternoon on the wooden deck of the Lakeside Café at Pacific Fair, exchanging musical titbits.

'Sandi and the Sunsetz are out of this world. She is so talented,' Rhonda raved. 'They're from Japan. I just love her.'

'I'm not so into bands with girl singers.' I popped the bubbles of froth on my vanilla milkshake with a candy-striped straw, while Rhonda sipped her coffee like a grown-up.

'The rest of the band are cute, and she's so cool ...'

'Too complicated,' I laughed. 'I'm intimidated enough by other fans, let alone real female rockers. Although maybe *we* should start a band,' I added, only half joking.

'Like the Go-Gos. I heard they started out as a bit of a Vulture Club themselves.'

'Really? The Go-Gos?'

'So the story go-goes.'

'I could play the keyboards.' It was the only instrument I was proficient at. 'But I'd rather be the lead singer. Like Debbie Harry or Joan Jett.'

'Wouldn't you rather play the pink saxophone?' Rhonda looked at me over her John Lennon sunglasses.

'Sicko.'

She stuck her tongue in her cheek and simulated a very lopsided blowjob.

We tucked into our plate of hot chips with vinegar, let the sun burn our arms and pulled out our little black books. We had bought each other matching notebooks with shiny gilt-edged pages. Like snazzy businesswomen we flipped them open and asked the waiter for a pen.

'What have you got?' she asked.

I shook my head and pulled a face.

'Not much. Lean pickings.' I drew doodles on my pages.

Rhonda slipped two plastic packets from her little backpack. They were sheets of adhesive stars, the sort teachers gave to primary-school kids for good work. She had gold, silver and green. We'd never found bronze ones, so green had to suffice. Then she pulled out a sheet of red ones.

'What are the red ones for?'

She laughed that demonic laugh of hers, crumbs of hot chips spraying back onto the plate.

'Guess?'

'I dunno ... for killing a rock star?'

'No, stupid. For doing more than one rock star at a time.'

My sunglasses clattered to the table. I stared at her and my mouth went dry.

'You didn't!'

She pulled a cryptic face, raised her eyebrows and then collapsed into laughter.

'NO!' Then she looked back up at me seriously. 'But I heard about someone who did. She did the whole band, in the same hotel room, in combinations that would make your teeth fall out.'

'I would never do that!' I'd read about orgies in *Cleo* but it sounded scary and potentially confusing. 'What about you?'

'Oh, I don't know. I guess it would depend.'

We both drifted into fantasyland, staring out at the ducks on the brown man-made lake. Rhonda threw the last few chips into the water and we watched them frenzy.

'They'd have to be pretty special,' Rhonda mused. 'Let's face it. Most bands have only got one or two good-looking guys and the rest are ugly mates along for the ride.'

'True,' I nodded, and we looked at one another and shouted, *'DRAGON!'*, linking pinkies and each making a silent wish for having said something simultaneously.

It was a running joke that Dragon was the ugliest band in Australia. Queen won the international title.

'But ugly guys can be very sexy.' Rhonda was suddenly serious. 'Really. I mean, you love Rod Stewart.'

I blew a stream of milkshake at her through my straw, the milk leaving a dribble down her cheek.

'He is *not* ugly.'

'He's not pretty.'

The waiter took away out plate of crumbs and salt.

'What do you think of that Brian guy in the Radiators?' I asked.

'Kind of sexy. But not exactly pretty.'

'Steve Kilbey's pretty,' I smiled indulgently.

'But not exactly sexy.'

'He is too!' I argued.

'David Lee Roth is pretty and sexy ... not!' Rhonda giggled.

'Hey ... all of Australian Crawl are pretty sexy,' I grinned.

'I dare you to "red star" them, then!'

'Never. Individually. At separate times. No problem. But all at once? What am I, an octopus?'

'An octopussy!' she yelled a bit too loudly.

Some young surfer guys were walking past in long hippy pants and crocheted string singlets. They were frowning at us. Rhonda gave them a wolf-whistle and they gave us the finger.

'Freaky punks!' they called.

'Idiots,' I laughed. 'They wouldn't know a punk if they tripped over one.'

'So what are we, then?' asked Rhonda.

'New-age babes? Rock chicks? Vultures?'

'Explorers.'

We went back to our little books and distributed the stars. We assessed our collection of names quarterly. Between us we had representatives of INXS, the Divinyls, Cold Chisel, Australian Crawl. A few local Gold Coast and Brisbane bands. Some gold. Some silver. A few greens. No reds.

'I'm counting crew as well,' Rhonda noted without pausing for discussion. 'They're extensions of the band.'

'I dunno about that.'

'Really. They are the backbone of the band. The flesh and blood. The band is just the hot air.'

'Who?' I asked, knowing she must have someone special in mind.

'Just a guy. He's crew and he's really, really nice.'

'No love!' I yelled at her. 'The code, remember? No feelings. Brutal notches on the belt!'

'He's just nice, that's all. Don't worry,' she said, looking away.

And then the inevitable happened. Lust and love don't always go together but, sooner or later, if you dally with one the two are bound to turn up in the same bed. Lust was the driving force behind the Vulture Club. Love was forbidden. It was as bad, if not worse, than a venereal disease. We had pledged that if we ever found ourselves doodling a musician's name after our own or forsaking some out of loyalty to one, we would walk away.

I broke that golden rule.

7.

In the faintly shabby three-star motel, we stood facing one another. He undressed me slowly. I undressed him. Our eyes remained locked. His handsome but world-weary face was hauntingly familiar. Not just *Countdown* or *Rolling Stone* familiar but resonant from some deep, dark, far-away place in another dimension. We stood staring at each other until he leaned forward and kissed me with such gentle abandon that it left me breathless. Electric and earthy at the same time, it was like I had never been kissed before. The sensations travelled from my mouth like an atomic bomb, mushrooming until they reached my toes, which curled into the cheap carpet.

He tasted of tea and bourbon.

Leading me to the bed, he pulled back the pale-blue chenille spread and sheets. We lay beside one another in a wordless suspension and I could feel the invisible charge between us. I was breathing, but barely. He rolled onto his side and let a warm finger trace my eyebrow. A dark fringe fell across his face.

'Why are you here with me?' he asked in a faintly British lilt, sweet and warm as honey. 'Is it because I'm famous?' A tiny smile curled at one corner of his mouth.

'No ... I ... no.' My voice came out as a whisper.

'Do you often fall into bed with musicians?' He ran that finger down my nose. My lips. My neck. My breast. It circled my nipple, which swelled up to meet him like a ripe strawberry.

'No.' I shut my eyes so that he couldn't see my lie.

I waited. Silence. Only the sound of his breath. His finger burned a trail over my body and I quivered gently at his touch.

'Am I your first?'

I froze, unable to answer. I couldn't lie again.

'No.' I opened my eyes to gauge his reaction.

He gave me an embracing smile.

'I want you to imagine that I am the first. Okay? Can you do that for me?'

I nodded, breathless, and died in his arms that night.

I made love for the first time and realised, at the tender age of almost seventeen, that there was a huge gulf between having sex and making love. Not fucking, but music. I cried with a jumble of joy and surprise. The astounding beauty of it had me spurting tears like a salty geyser and he held me until I thought my heart might be squeezed in half. I was lost and found in the same gasping breath.

As the first purple tentacles of light appeared through the venetian blinds I dressed, watching him sleep, his pale skin melting into the sheets, his mop of dark, coarse hair haloed about the pillow. Eyelashes so childlike. Lips puffing invisible cigarettes. My body itched for more of him and the tenderness I felt in my heart radiated to my inner thighs.

I did what I had never done before and left my phone number on a sheet of paper by the bed, crested with the name of the motel. I added the words, 'Thank you. That was beautiful,' then walked home through the new morning. I drizzled like a spring shower all the way.

Feigning illness that day I stayed home in bed, waiting for him to call.

He didn't.

And thus I began a post-coital degree in my new lover, researching everything I could about him. I read the lyrics to every one of the songs he had written and irrationally related them all to our evening of passion. I walked around in a daze of distraction. I couldn't eat. I considered taking up smoking. I struggled to wake up from fitful sleep, not interested in leaving my dreams of him. I wrote his name next to mine and drew fussy hearts. I sat at the piano and learned to play his band's ballads. I sang and could hear his voice silently harmonising with mine. His songs were beautiful and his voice as deep as a cold, black gorge. He was more than a musician. He was a poet.

My seventeenth birthday came and went with a quiet family dinner. The little ones enjoyed the cake and candles, but I was tormented by my fantasies. With a gaggle of friends I went to UB40 in town. I enjoyed the reggae beat but didn't wear my Vulture hat that night. I was grooving to the sound of faithful monogamy. I was appalled and proud of myself at the same time.

Three weeks later he rang.

For three weeks I had rehearsed witty dialogue in anticipation of this moment but instead we slipped easily into a comfortable silliness. He raved about the injustices of record producers, Kentucky Fried Chicken and the white slave trade, and I deduced that he was a little stoned. When he finally began to make sense he told me he'd be back at the same motel the following Friday and invited me to a party.

I lay on my bed, replaying his every word in my head. Five days. I tried to calculate the hours. Five times twenty-four. I gave up and rolled over to press the play button on my ghetto blaster. His voice had my hands roaming into practice positions.

It was a long and tedious wait. I prayed to Jimi Hendrix and Elvis and all the dead saints of rock and roll: *Nothing go wrong. Nothing go wrong.* My younger sister, Annie, three years my junior, was an enterprising smart-arse, always on the lookout for opportunities to meddle. She wore deceptively innocent dark braids on either side of her face, like Pocahontas, and insisted she would one day join a nunnery. I had bet her one hundred dollars she wouldn't, but it seemed an unwinnable bet: she had a lifetime to prove me wrong. I should have set a time limit.

Friday night at last. Clear skies. Parents' lights out. Slinky black pants and black T-shirt with nice boob curvature. Flat black shoes. Simple dark eyes and pale lips. Skin surprisingly pimple-free. Check. Check. Check. I was just about to launch out the window when my bedroom door opened and Sister Annie of the Immaculate Pain in the Bum stood in the doorway, hands on hips.

'Where are you off to?' she sneered with the calm elation of someone who knows she's got the goods on you.

'I'm ... ah ... just dressing up ... trying out some looks ...' I stuttered.

'The window?' she asked steadily.

'It ... ahh ... I was going to clean it ... I ...'

'This is the ninth time you've disappeared that I know of. You don't get home until about five in the morning.'

'Oh come on, Annie ... what do I have to do? What do you want? Please – can we talk about it tomorrow?'

'Ten dollars a night.' She smiled with her perfect teeth.

I baulked.

'That's my entire allowance!'

'Five, then.'

She had me.

'Fine, but starting next time.'

She nodded and gave a little wave.

'They won't pay you this well in the bloody convent,' I hissed after her.

She gave me the finger and closed my door without a sound.

I walked fast that night and arrived at the hotel, the Hibiscus or Poinsettia Views or some such. Skirting the pool, I followed the noise to the second floor and walked along the balcony toward Room 36, where people, smoke and music were spilling out into the night. Deep breath. Quick breast rearrangement. Last finger-tease of my hair.

Pushing through the crowd, I found my lover sitting cross-legged in the middle of the floor, a circle of ebony-clad followers around him. He wore an orange crocheted tea cosy on his head and a fine rim of eyeliner around his piercing eyes, giving him a wolfish look. When he saw me he hooted.

'Persephone, my love.' He waved frantically at me as if trying to scare off a bug. The room swirled with acrid smoke. Somewhere a woman was squealing like a Chihuahua being neutered and someone smashed a glass at the exact moment I sat down beside him and accepted a passionate kiss. It was an appropriate percussional accompaniment.

'This is my new muse,' he called to the room of revellers. A few nods and waves. Someone passed me a joint and I declined. Another touched his nose and nodded toward the bathroom. This was a different sort of crowd from the one I was used to. More sinister somehow. I felt out of place and my beautiful poet noticed immediately.

'You have not been introduced to the mysteries of the weed, have you my love?'

I had smoked the odd Alpine cigarette but had never touched anything harder than a little booze.

'Why did you call me Persephone?' Had he forgotten my name?

'The tears of the innocent, my love.' He touched my brow with his finger and leaned in close, putting his high forehead to mine.

'You are coming with me. Don't worry. It's only early and I can get you to Neverland and back before first light. Okay?' he whispered.

He smelled like a burnt eucalyptus forest. I agreed without missing a beat.

He pulled me to my feet and we pushed through the crush, out into the fresh air. I was light-headed from just a few minutes in the motel room. Celebrity-hungry leeches flung themselves at my Poet, but he put his head down and dragged me behind him like a sail.

We tripped and tumbled through Cavill Avenue toward the beach. Drunken youths staggered and shouted insults at one another. Women sheathed in white cheesecloth and gold costume jewellery flounced out of restaurants, their arthritic husbands shuffling behind them.

'Where are we going?' I laughed.

He stopped and turned with a flourish.

'We're going to paradise. The sign says so.' He pointed theatrically up at the shoddy unlit sign: 'Surfers Paradise Beach'. Two McDonald's pickles clung to it and someone had spray-painted a penis onto the smiling cartoon sun.

Taking off our shoes, we left them on the top step and climbed down to the beach. Like kids we ran to the water's edge before walking north, away from the main drag.

'Here,' he announced after a while and we plonked ourselves down on the damp sand.

An almost full moon shimmered yellow over the silvery sea. The rhythmic swoosh of water meeting sand and then withdrawing was soothing. Each breath filled my nose with the kelpy smell of the surf.

From his top pocket the Poet pulled a joint and like a magician produced a small burst of flame from his other hand. He lit the twisted paper and it crackled and flared. After a few moments he put it to my lips.

'Just a little. Don't burn your throat,' he cautioned.

I drew a little smoke into my mouth but found it much denser and hotter than a normal cigarette. I coughed and tried again. After only a few seconds I felt softly dizzy. My muscles seemed to melt. There was a tingling in my fingers and toes and a strange numbness massaged my face.

'Hmmm.'

The Poet finished the smoke and then he began to sing. He sang about the moon and crooned to me by name, which quelled my worries about being called Persephone.

'I love your voice. It's magic.' I rested my head on his shoulder affectionately.

'I love your teeth. Can I lick them?' I drew back and squinted at him to see if he was mocking me, but his sparkling eyes reassured me.

'Sure,' I giggled and lay back on the sand, and we kissed. His tongue lapped at each tooth and danced across my tongue and our lips nuzzled and nudged, exploring. Finally we fell apart and stared up at the Milky Way.

'The dentist did an x-ray and said I don't have any wisdom teeth,' I announced.

'That's because you are so wise already, far wiser than your ... how many years?'

He turned his face toward me. I had never told any of my conquests how old I really was. The Poet was older than my other lovers but tonight I felt inspired and told him the truth.

'I'm seventeen.'

He rolled back onto the sand and let out a huge breath, like a deflating balloon. I waited. The blood in my brain banged like a runaway timpani.

And then he began to sing again, softly and slowly.

'Well she was just seventeen. You know what I mean ... ' He leapt to his feet and began a wild Beatles corroboree on the sand, singing at the top of his voice. I jumped up and we sang and danced like a couple of swinging sixties kids. 'Well she looked at me, and I, I could see—'

Suddenly a voice boomed from behind a sand dune in the darkness.

'Shut the hell up! I'm trying to get laid here.'

We screamed with laughter and ran north along the water's edge, zigzagging as if we were avoiding bullets. I was elated. My feet seemed to miss every second step. Almost flying. I was in Neverland.

After however long we stopped and doubled over, breathless with laughter. We sat on the sand and soon we were entwined, our warm breaths merging. There were suddenly no stars, no water and no sand. Just the Poet and me and the blood-beat hammering through our veins.

I let him undress me and I lay on the cool sand completely naked, spread out like a starfish, without embarrassment. In the moonlight I had no freckles. I was a Greek statue made of marble. The Poet undressed himself and ran toward the water, calling out to me to follow. The *Jaws* theme filled my head but I raced after his lean body, my breasts bouncing against my chest, and plunged into the black and silver waves.

We splashed and frolicked like young seals, buffeted by choppy breakers. The tender skin of my hip took a scrape from the gravelly seabed and I thought I'd swallowed a jelly fish after being dumped open-mouthed.

At last we crawled out of the primordial sea and landed together in the shallows. The water tickled my skin and I lay back and let the frothy suds wash my hair with briny slop. We made love again, perfectly in tune, the sea splashing gently against us like applause.

At one stage a couple walked by hand in hand and someone called out to us, 'Nice night for it.' We laughed into each other's matted hair, our concentration only momentarily broken. If anyone else came upon us, we didn't notice.

'From here to eternity,' he whispered.

As we lay satisfied in the water, I couldn't believe a night could be so magical.

I left the Poet at a taxi rank on the corner of Cavill Avenue and the highway. Sand grated between my thighs, I smelled like a fish and eyeliner blurred the underbellies of my eyes. He leaned in the cab window, looking like a wild sea anemone, and thrust a twenty-dollar note and two joints into my hand.

'Sweet dreams, Persephone,' he grinned and disappeared. As I settled in for the drive home the driver frowned disapprovingly into his rear-vision mirror.

I felt something unusual. A sea nymph had taken over my soul. I called it love.

8.

In March 1983, Labor swept into office with Bob Hawke at the helm. My dad was over the moon. We dutifully studied the election in modern history class, but the details left me cold. The Senate. The ballot. The lower house. Where was my delicious Poet?

He had mentioned he would be heading for Europe before too long. I marvelled at how little I knew about him. Who was he? What was his favourite food? What made him smile? What was he afraid of? I wanted to study the history of him. Everything else swirled past my ears like dandelion fluff, utterly unimportant.

It was a hot March. The pavement blistered like a barbecue grill. The nation was still numb with shock after February's Ash Wednesday fires and the threat of more hung over the hinterland like a spectre. Sweat trickled between my shoulderblades and I imagined the Poet's tongue lapping at my salty skin. In class, I put my head down on the desk and shut my eyes, letting the talk of parliaments and preferences wash over me. I woke up ten minutes later with saliva dribbling down my chin. Kids bumped and kicked my chair as they shuffled out of the classroom.

'Wake up, Sleeping Beauty,' my teacher sighed. 'Make sure you hand that essay in tomorrow.'

By now the Vulture Club was little more than an occasional phone call, but my friendship with Sam had deepened and I felt I could confide in her. Pouring out my feelings for the Poet, I plied her with details of my midnight antics. She loved it. 'Tell me more' became her greeting to me every morning.

On the Monday after my briny second encounter with the Poet, I bailed Sam up at morning tea and breathlessly told her I'd brought a joint to school.

'I'm up for it, if you are,' she said, cocking an eyebrow.

'Where, though?' I wondered.

During ancient history class, Sam came up with a brilliant and possibly insane idea: we would smoke it in the staff toilets near the library.

'All the teachers will be at lunch,' she whispered. 'The librarians have their lunch down the other end of the building and there's a toilet down there as well ... so for at least the first fifteen minutes we'll have the place to ourselves.' Her plan was sound and getting sounder. 'Plus, the window opens out over the car park, not the playground. There's no-one out there, ever.' We nodded and the time was fixed.

It became a mission of exact precision. We went in one at a time to smoke, while the other stood guard at the door with a book. During sentry changes the crumpled joint sat perched on the edge of the basin, smoking itself. We contorted ourselves, standing on a toilet seat, in order to blow all the smoke out the high window.

It was only after we'd rinsed our mouths and returned to the library that the intense paranoia set in. They'd smell it. Someone had seen us go in. Our eyes were red. We found the most inane things amusing and our laughter took on a life of its own, sabotaging our ridiculous efforts to appear 'straight'. Every frown thrown our way was a direct accusation and eventually we took refuge in the darkroom, giggling until the photography teacher sent us outside with a camera. We ran about accosting people and screaming 'Smile!', and returned with a selection of portraits of startled students and staff.

The next few weeks passed uneventfully. I had no interest whatsoever in going out. The walk to Surfers had become tiresome and repetitive and after my romance with the Poet, it felt wrong to chase other musicians. When I told Rhonda this by phone, she said I was obviously unwell and should take a few aspirins, lie down and wait for it to pass. She also suggested I should ditch the Poet.

'He's bad news. Get yourself back to an Aussie Crawl gig. That'll knock some sense into you.'

Sister Annie was irritable. She was used to earning five dollars a night but now I was on hiatus.

'You should go out again. Give me three dollars and I won't tell. Goanna is playing at Bombay Rock tomorrow night.'

I narrowed my eyes at her. She knew more about my adventures than she should. I wondered if she'd found my diary, wedged beneath my mattress.

'What do you spend all this money on, Annie? You're not on drugs, are you?' I teased.

'Holy cards from the presbytery shop.' She smiled like a lizard.

We were arguing this way one afternoon when Mum came into my room behind Annie and threw me one of her 'you're in trouble' looks.

'I renewed these ridiculous magazines once and I can't do it again. They're overdue.' She glared at me, but I had no idea what she was talking about.

'Pardon, Mum?'

'The library! I'm not going to pay your fines. Your pop magazines.' She read from the library notice in her hand. 'Two *Countdown* magazines and three *Rolling Stones*. Rubbish. They've been out for more than five weeks now. I renewed them at two weeks and now they're overdue again. Are you listening, Nikki? Dad's driving to Pacific Fair and he'll drop them back on the way.'

I opened my mouth to speak but nothing came out so I nodded dumbly. A deep sense of dread began to creep up my legs. A memory. Pedalling my too-small bike to the Broadbeach library to research the Poet after our monumental tryst. And then another memory. I had come home at breakneck speed because my period had made an appearance at the library and I'd been unprepared. That seemed a long time ago. Too long.

Pulling the magazines from the top drawer of my bedside table, I looked at the stamps on the front pages. Some quick calculations. Not good. I grabbed a piece of paper and counted out each day with a tick, just to double-check. Every day from then until now. One week. Two weeks. A little over five weeks.

I was late. I was overdue. My first period had trickled into my life at the age of twelve and for five years I'd been like clockwork. Twenty-seven or twenty-eight days. Never thirty-seven. I felt like I'd crested a roller-coaster and come racing down hard. People were late all the time, I was sure. It couldn't always be exact. Surely.

With a good deal of stealth and even more terror, I stole into the dining room and put the magazines on the table. Trying to look casual, I scoured the well-stocked bookcases, looking for Mum's copy of *Everywoman: A gynaecological guide for life*. This book had played a large part in my sex self-education and its sketch of an erect penis was a lasting memory from my early teens. I had pawed over the illustrations of various sexual positions and richly fantasised. It had been my first taste of educational pornography but this afternoon I needed a different kind of help. Finally I found its blue spine and whipped it out in one razor-sharp manoeuvre, sticking it up my T-shirt and racing back to the safety of my room. I hadn't had sex in over three weeks. It had been in the surf. Surely that was safe. An instant douche!

I read and read and did not like what I found. I had been with the Poet mid-cycle, which was the most fertile time. Shit. Shit. Shit! My lips quivered and my breath came in little dry gasps. Symptoms. Symptoms. Tender breasts. I squeezed. Ouch. Fuck. They were heavy and definitely sore. Deep purple labia. I grabbed my hand mirror, pulled down my undies and stood as if I were attempting the splits. Jesus Christ! I reeled a little. I wasn't expecting to look like that. I guess it was kind of purple. I'd never looked before. I squinted and peered again. How ironic that I had seen more than a baker's dozen of penises but never a real live vagina, not even my own. What a bizarre arrangement, I thought, replacing the mirror on the dressing table. I stared ahead into the larger mirror and tried to look within myself. I leaned forward and studied my face. Did I look different? Yes. I looked ... I looked ... terrified.

All I knew of pregnancy I had learned from the gestations of my two youngest siblings. Rachel was born when I was ten and David when I was twelve. I had enjoyed the days before their births, sitting on the end of Mum's bed, going through baby-name books. As a little girl I'd had Barbie dolls, but I'd never been charmed by baby dolls or cribs or bottles and nappies. I used to chop my dolls' hair off, subject them to tragic deaths and bury them in the backyard. Our back lawn was littered with Barbie carcasses. I was appalled by baby poop – that orange mustard – and had worn my fair share of it during my little siblings' first years. I remembered warmly my dad's ecstatic reaction to the birth of his only son. The two of us had sat up in the wee hours after Dad returned from the hospital. We ate half a pig of bacon and Dad told me how brave Mum had been and how beautiful David was. I had changed nappies. I had held bottles. I'd cuddled and loved my little siblings and I'd always assumed I'd be a mother one day – but I hadn't planned for that day to be in 1983.

My first line of defence was denial. Any twinge of pain in my gut must be an early sign of menstruation. I did fifty starjumps a day, hoping to shake something loose. I checked the gusset of my knickers like a woman possessed, inserting a testing finger at every opportunity. My finger came up clean and the fabric remained unstained. I tempted fate by wearing white pants and leaving the house without tampons. Pale blue veins appeared on my breasts and I began to spend more time in the loo – not just for checking purposes, but because my bladder seemed suddenly to have the capacity of a thimble.

Fear began to take hold. This was one situation I could not just ignore away. I scanned the back of the Poet's LP, searching for a way to contact him. Rock stars did not give out their phone numbers. I scribbled down the names of managers and record company executives, having no real idea how to track him down. Besides, I didn't want to tell him the news until I knew for sure what I was dealing with. A trip to a doctor seemed unavoidable but I was fearful that my parents would have to be told. My life was an elevator and the walls were closing in.

I confided in Sam. Her blue eyes gaped and her mouth contorted like a giant clam.

'Tell me more ... ' she whispered, although there was no-one within earshot. She held my hand as I cried silently, searching for words.

'But you're not sure?' she prompted gently.

I shook my head, noisily sniffing back tears.

'Well, let's find out. I'll wag English and buy you a test from the chemist. I got paid yesterday,' she offered. She had a part-time job, cleaning the offices of the *Gold Coast Bulletin*. A reluctant smile was all I could muster by way of gratitude.

Although I was not quite two weeks overdue, we took a chance on the test. Pale yellow urine sloshed about the bottom of a Styrofoam cup and we waited, both of us, watching the tiny plastic window of the tester. No positive plus sign and I will go back to church. I will never have sex again. I'll give all my allowance to the poor or to Annie. I will never, ever crawl out my window again. I will become a nun. Anything.

But no. The universe was a bastard and the blue cross blinked back at us. We looked at one another. Time stood still. Slowly I emptied the cup into the basin and gave it a rinse, staring at the water gushing from the steel tap. At that moment I wished I could be swirled away along with the condemning juices from my bladder.

Out in the blinding sunlight, Sam put her arm around me and we sat down under our favourite ghost gum. Its papery bark lay stripped and ragged around us. I picked at my fingernails, chewing on them anxiously.

'They won't do it in Queensland,' Sam said, breaking the silence.

I looked up at her bleakly.

'It's illegal. But you can go down to Tweed Heads. I knew someone who knew someone who did it last year.'

Tweed Heads was just over the border in New South Wales. There was no other option. We were living under the draconian regime of Premier Joh Bjelke-Petersen, a self-righteous fellow who had also outlawed condom vending machines. I had heard about a clinic in Brisbane but Sam thought it had been shut down after a raid.

I thought about my lover and felt a wave of nausea.

'I have to tell him.'

'No!' Sam slapped a hand over my mouth for such blasphemy. 'No. If you really do like this guy, you can't tell him. You'll never see him again.'

'He might ... he might ...'

'Don't even think about it.'

A pensive silence blanketed us.

'I'll come with you,' Sam ventured at last. 'It's not even as bad as having a tooth pulled, I heard.'

A son or a daughter. It was inconceivable. I imagined I could feel a pulse. A throbbing growth. I stopped myself with a sharp intake of breath. I could not allow myself to think like that. In my guts I knew that there was only one solution.

This was not a baby. Not a life. This was a tragic consequence of my lack of precaution. Rarely did a musician ask me if I was on the pill. It was always an unspoken assumption. I had been too afraid to approach a doctor. I didn't have enough money and I was terrified my parents would find out. I kept a secret diary but it was largely in a code only I could understand. If my parents discovered evidence that I was sexually active, I would never be absolved. For a Catholic girl, nothing was more important than chastity.

Money was a major problem. Disappearing was not an option. I had nowhere to run to. Abortion was my only option.

This I accepted with a heavy sadness, pushing away thoughts of the love, beauty and life that were not on offer to me.

'How much does it cost?' I asked in a monotone.

'Not sure. We'll ring up and ask. There are numbers in the yellow pages.' She smiled compassionately.

'You know all this ... how?'

'I read a story in *Cosmo*.'

Well, that'll be a valuable source of information, I thought cynically.

'I should tell him.'

'Why?' She looked at me intensely. 'What good would that do? He'll just call you a groupie ... how would he even know it was his? He'll run a mile.'

'It is his,' I sulked. 'No wonder it was so bloody good. It was ... surreal.'

'You were stoned.'

'It wasn't just that. I wasn't stoned the first time. There's some mystical connection between us.'

'You're hormonal and mad.' She shook her head. 'Trust me. We'll scam some money. You go down next weekend and in half an hour you'll be all fixed up and next time this guy's in town you can screw him senseless again.' She patted me maternally on the knee. 'Only this time, you'll be on the pill. Agreed?'

I knew I had to be sensible.

'Agreed.'

There was a pause while we sat, almost in prayer. The ants ran up the white trunk of the ghost gum and an Ibis ran from behind the tree.

'We'll have a raffle. We'll raise the money with a raffle.'

I laughed for the first time in a week.

I thought she'd been joking but within a week, she'd raised the funds I needed and I'd made an appointment with a small private clinic south of the border. The kids who bought raffle tickets were told they'd go into a draw to win 'Three Completed Top-quality Assignments in Subjects of Your Choice', and that they were helping to fund a top-secret mission Sam and I were on. They probably figured we wanted to buy drugs or a new wardrobe or some such thing. It seemed a fair exchange to them.

Against Sam's advice, I did what I could to contact the Impregnating Poet. I rang his management office and left a message for him to call me. The woman I spoke to was not pleasant enough to be called polite. She took my name and number but I could almost hear her crumple it up and slam-dunk it into the waste-paper bin before she hung up. I did manage to learn that he was 'somewhere in the UK'. She asked me not to call that number again.

With pain, I realised this was my problem alone. There was no relationship. We had no 'future'. It was time to cut my losses and deal with the hand I had been given.

My appointment was for Friday morning. I had never been able to play truant from school because my father was on staff, but as luck would have it he was in Brisbane at a professional development seminar for the whole week. Someone in the other world was looking after me. Elvis? John Lennon? I listened to *Double Fantasy*, Lennon's final album, a lot that week.

Disaster struck on Wednesday. Early in the morning, Sam rang, very upset, and explained that a death in the family meant she and her mother were flying to Sydney for a week. Could I really go through this alone? Sam suggested I ask another friend to come, but I wanted no-one else. Okay, not true. I wanted the Poet beside me. I shut my eyes, called upon all my strength and assured her I would be fine. I put the phone down and squeezed my hands together. I'd never understood what it meant to 'wring one's hands with worry' until then.

9.

Friday morning came. I had lain awake all night, listening to the fruit bats nibbling the date tree outside my bedroom window. They would squeak and scratch and every now and then a date would hit the ground with a thud. Thirty-nine fell that night. I felt like a five-year-old on Christmas Eve or a condemned prisoner on death row, excited and afraid but craving release from my misery. I was scared to sleep for fear of dreaming of a happy future with my Poet and 2.3 little poets, a white sedan and a well-behaved golden retriever.

At 5.06 a.m. sunlight finally shone though the crack between the curtains. I had packed my schoolbag with a change of clothes and the sanitary napkins the clinic nurse had told me to bring. I had smuggled two Panadol tablets from the medicine cabinet. The nurse had suggested I might need them, as pain relief was not included in the price of the procedure.

I caught the bus from the corner opposite the shops, as I did whenever Dad was not giving me a lift. But as we turned left at the chicken shop at the end of Monaco Street I got off, telling the driver I'd left an important assignment at home. He shrugged. He didn't give a crap. I was over-informing out of paranoia. I changed in the public toilets at the service station and sat waiting for the bus to Tweed Heads, hoping no-one who knew my mother drove past.

The journey was slow, an endless staccato of stops and starts, and I kept checking the watch Mum had given me for my seventeenth birthday. I could have sworn the second hand stopped whenever I looked away.

Finally we were in New South Wales. After a long, hot walk from the bus stop I arrived opposite the clinic, a pale-blue building. Crossing the road I walked straight into a group of three people – two women and a man – unpacking signs. I stared at the words and felt a cold wave of dread pass over me. Guilt washed the colour from my face and I tried to shake it off but it was too late. They had seen. I moved away, mumbling an apology, but one of the women grabbed my wrist.

'You have other options, sweetheart. If you'll give us just a couple of minutes ...'

The man pulled a little plastic thing from his pocket and held it up in front of my face. It looked like the Hang Ten surf-gear logo. It was a pair of skin-coloured feet.

'Your baby has feet this size or bigger.' He did not sound as friendly as the woman. 'You look far too nice to be a murderer.' His eyes blazed and his pate shone and I stared at him, unable to craft words of rebuttal.

'I'm sorry.' I made for the clinic.

'Does your mother know you're here?' a woman's angry voice called from behind me but I did not look back.

'Jesus loves you,' the man shouted. His voice was full of hate. I shut my eyes, took a deep breath and turned to face them.

'If Jesus loves me now, he'll still love me when I come out of here.'

I blocked out their sudden singing and hurried through the heavy frosted-glass doors. The air conditioning seemed too cold and I walked across to the receptionist, conscious of the squeak my school shoes made on the floor. There was no-one at all in the waiting area, to my relief.

The brunette at the desk was as efficient as Pine-o-Clean

and gave me a refreshing smile. With hyperactive friendliness she took my details and asked me to pay up-front. The price I'd been quoted over the phone did not include a general anaesthetic, she explained, just a light local anaesthetic. She gave me a receipt, took down my Medibank number, assured me it would all be confidential and asked me to take a seat.

Not two minutes later another emphatically positive woman appeared and called me by my first name. We retired to her comfortable office. After a little small talk she got down to more serious business.

'Are you in a relationship with the father?'

'I don't know ... he's in England or somewhere like that. He's a bit ... quite a bit older than me and it ... I've only been with him a couple of times ...' I blushed, never having spoken to an adult woman about my active sex life.

'Have you discussed this with your parents or a teacher or someone who can support you after the procedure?'

'There's Sam. She's my best friend. She was going to be here but something came up ...' I shrugged and gave a pained smile. 'My parents would kill me. Literally.'

'What would upset them more? The fact that you are having sex or the fact that you have decided to have a termination?'

'Both ... I don't know. Yeah, both, I suppose. They're Catholic.'

'If you had to give me your primary reason for making this choice today, what would it be?'

How to narrow it down to just one? I measured my answer and tried to put my many reasons into some kind of order.

'Well, I'm too young and I don't think the father would be ... around for me very much and I don't have family support for something like this and ... I want to do something with my life. I've got nothing to give a baby and that just wouldn't be fair. If I do this, I can still have a life. If I had a baby now, I think ... really ... I'd be wrecking two lives.'

Not long later, after an examination by a doctor and a blood test, I was dressed in a white smock open at the back, lying on a hard examination table. I'd been given a Valium tablet and felt a little light-headed. From outside I could hear muffled voices and my legs quivered with goosebumps. I was having crazy thoughts: What if there is a God and he is going to be seriously pissed off with me now? What if I bleed to death? What if ... if ... if?

The doctor strode in, dressed in pale-blue scrubs, and a nurse followed. She too wore a cheesy grin and I wondered if it was compulsory for the female staff.

'Okay, then,' the doctor began. 'Sherilyn here will explain the procedure as we go so you understand what you are feeling and why. Are we all set? We'll take about fifteen minutes.'

My legs were placed into uncomfortable stirrups and I felt like a dartboard as Dr Whatshisname aimed his syringe and Sherilyn gave me a running commentary. First came the local anaesthetic to the cervix. It was like no pain I'd ever felt. I can only liken it to having a red-hot needle pushed though your eyeball, slowly. The rest of the ordeal was just as bad and felt more like an hour than fifteen minutes. The sound of a suction device made my skin crawl and nausea hit me like a tsunami. Cramping and stinging and feeling like a piece of meat being carved up in a butcher's shop, I clenched my teeth and swore off sex for life. Half an hour later I was bleeding into a pad, sipping a hot cup of tea and forcing down a chocolate biscuit. I'd swallowed my Panadol and tried to focus on a *New Idea* magazine, to little avail.

An hour later I was on the bus home. I'd been shunned by the pro-lifers out the front on my way out. I was beyond salvation by that stage, I suppose – a condemned murderer. Finally the coast road's shabby shops, fibro shacks and used-car yards made way for the more cosmopolitan ugliness of the Gold Coast and I was back at the corner of Monaco Street, being accosted by a man in a chicken suit offering two cooked chooks for the price of one. I changed back into my uniform at the servo and as I headed out of the car park Chicken Man called after me, 'Who's been a naughty girl, then? What was more fun than school, eh?'

I wanted to yell back, 'An abortion, you stupid chicken-shit arsehole!' but I just kept walking. I was tired. I was sore. I wanted to go to sleep for a very long time. My upper thighs felt like they were turning inside out and my womb was weeping painfully. I imagined this was something like what it felt like to be pack-raped. My feelings for the Poet had quite suddenly soured.

10.

I slept and slept. Dreamless unconsciousness. Shuffling through school days like an automaton, I spent lunchtimes in the library, trying in vain to study for the end of semester exams. Sam said she was worried about me. I told her not to bother. The emotional slump demanded peace and solitude.

The Tweed Heads ordeal had been a wake-up call. I was not playing some silly party game like Pin the Tail on the Rock God. My parents' Catholicism was not the root of my anguish. It was the fear that I had acted rashly and hormonally without properly thinking things through. I had made the only responsible choice, I repeated to myself often. But there was something so sad and disappointing about my first brush with motherhood.

Don't look back. You should never look back. Yet I kept looking over my shoulder, wallowing in what might have been. What would I have called a child? Something wild, like 'Ramone', or sensible, like 'Sarah'? Would he or she have had my freckles and frizzy hair or the Poet's brown eyes and lanky intensity? Had I told him, would he have gone down on bended knee and offered me a lifetime of loyalty and love? Had I told my parents, might they have understood and supported me? I began to fear that I had, perhaps, jumped the gun. Maybe there had been other options. Lamenting my position, I flipped through countless tomes on the ethics of life and death. I tried to make peace with myself but the harder I sought it the more elusive it became.

The doctor at the clinic had given me a prescription for the contraceptive pill and I swallowed it dutifully each morning. The pack was wedged deep inside my mattress, deposited through a small cut made with a kitchen knife. Although I swore I'd never have sex again, I still dreamed longing, lusty dreams about the Poet. When *Countdown* magazine ran an exclusive interview with him I let my fingers trace his handsome face on the glossy paper. He looked straight through me and I wondered if he'd given me the same generic sultry look he gave to the camera. Had he had sex with me the way another star might give an autograph? The more I analysed my two Poetic adventures, the lower my self-esteem sank. An inner voice taunted that I was about as meaningful to the Poet as a used condom – useful for a time but then distasteful, good for nothing but the rubbish bin. I began to hate him with a strange intensity, laced with passion and desire and deep, cancerous pain.

By the July school holidays, an uneasy anaesthesia had settled upon me. Nothing felt good anymore. There was nothing to look forward to or hope for. Sleep was my only escape and yet I would wake in the silence of the early morning and stare at nothing for hours on end. Once my sleepless hours had been filled with fantasies about sex, travel and fame. Now I spent them wading through brain fog.

Tiny sores like mosquito bites had appeared on my arms and legs and I picked at them relentlessly, digging at my flesh until they became infected and puss-filled. I stopped teasing my hair and walked with the hunched shoulders of a chronic asthmatic. Acne decorated my face and my eyes were hemmed with red. The smallest thing would bring on tears – a snap from my mother, a sigh from my father, a jibe from my sister or a concerned question from friends, all of whom I tried to hide from. Food bored me and I began sneaking cigarettes from my parents and smoking them behind the house when they were out. I detested smoking but I detested not smoking more. I moped about, showering only when it became absolutely necessary and picking at dry toast instead of real food. I think my parents assumed it was all some histrionic teenage nonsense.

I tried to slice through my numbness by cutting myself deeply. A dull sensation radiated up my arm and I watched a rivulet of blood slide down over my wrist. There was still no pain.

Not with a bang but a whimper. Perhaps the most pivotal decisions are made, not in the heat of the moment or during a profound epiphany, but from a place of simple surrender. One day I woke up and the sludge just seemed a little sludgier. The heavy sense of foreboding had become an ounce too burdensome and so I raised my hands to heaven and said, 'Enough.'

There was no cry for help, no adolescent bravado, just a submissive acceptance of what was for the best. I did not beat my chest and demand to be released from my suffering. I simply determined one Friday evening that my lack of élan was no longer tolerable and I decided to die.

While my mother bathed the two youngest children and Dad sat in the family room, ears plugged into Billy Joel, I undertook a stealth mission to my parents' medicine cabinet. It was a pharmaceutical treasure chest, holding all manner of antidepressants and sleeping tablets. Many had never been opened, as though somebody had filled prescriptions but never taken the drugs. Perhaps they were someone else's back-up plan.

I pocketed about twenty pills, a cocktail of Serepax and Valium and something else that started with the letter S. I took them to my room with a jug of water and a glass. A soft feeling of serenity washed over me and I smiled. For the first time since Tweed Heads I felt at peace.

My desk was buried under a mountain of schoolwork. The exams were approaching that would supposedly set the course of my future. I was happy to let all that go.

One by one, I swallowed the bitter little dots. Goodbye, Oscar. Bon voyage, Hollywood and New York, New York. Arrivederci, rock stars. Blurred and hazy. Mum walking in. Getting me to my feet. I fell heavily to the bed. Voice. Mum. Angry. Trouble. Dark in the city. Night is a wire. Oblivion.

Two days later, I came back from the dead. As Lazarus I had one hell of a headache. Dragging my heavy carcass from the sweat-soaked bed, I opened my curtains and could not tell what time of day it was. Pale blue haloed the gum trees beyond the neighbour's fence. Dawn or dusk? My tongue was swollen and limped about my mouth, seeking moisture like a parched leech.

Quietly I skulked to the bathroom and washed. A change of clothes and a toothbrush livened me up a little. My bed sheets needed stripping and I went so far as to open the window and invite in fresh air and light. The yellowing of the sky confirmed it was early morning and I sat cross-legged on my bed, breathing deeply, eyes shut, listening to the rowdy birdlife outside. Two possibilities – either I was an idiot who couldn't pull off a simple overdose, or divine provenance had stepped in to save my damn life.

Perhaps it was not my time to go. Was there some grand purpose I was meant to fulfil? There was the Oscar. I still felt fame was my destiny. Why did I need this? Why did I feel so out of place and misunderstood? Why couldn't I just want what everyone else wanted? Why couldn't I be who my parents wanted me to be? Had collecting famous sexual partners been a form of vampirism? Was I trying to sap some of their fame DNA? I was a sexual kleptomaniac.

There was no way around it: I wanted to be in film and I wanted to be famous. Maybe this shallow dream *was* driven by feelings of inadequacy – for all my swagger, I was often shy and had a pathological fear of confrontation – but it was my dream nonetheless. How to get there with my terrible teeth was the conundrum. Oscar had a penchant for flashy gnashers. I would need extensive cosmetic dental work if I were to compete with the Brooke Shields and Farrah Fawcetts of the world. My teeth, God bless them, were strong and healthy and without so much as a rumour of a cavity – but they looked like God had poked them higgledy-piggledy into my gums after a big night out. If ever I complained about them to my parents I was scolded for vanity and reminded how lucky I was to have such healthy choppers.

Money, money, money. All the things I could do … if I had a little money. I sat, that post-suicidal morning, trying to think how I could raise the funds to renovate my smile and follow my dream to New York. I realised I might have to accept a longer timeframe than instantly, but no amount of shifts at McDonald's was ever going to do it. Anyway, I'd tried Maccas when I was fourteen. I'd been sacked at the beginning of 1981 for trying to kiss customers on New Year's Eve.

The answer came like a comet, jetting out of the newspaper classifieds. I sat at the breakfast table, my black-ringed eyes only inches from the tablecloth. My parents danced about tersely on silent tiptoes and I could tell Vesuvius was about to erupt. My close call had made me somewhat less interested in the small-time drama of the generation gap. Ignoring their discomfort, I let my finger touch a small advertisement.

'Guitar lessons. Former Skyhooks guitarist. Beginners welcome.'

The Skyhooks were the biggest rock act of the seventies. That's it! a voice screamed in my head. Eureka. Don't be a groupie – be a rock star. The Go-Gos. The Bangles. Cyndi Lauper. Suzie Quatro. Blondie. I could play gigs. Make money. Get famous.

But my strobe-lit fantasy dimmed as the recriminations began.

'We are so disappointed in you,' began my father through tight lips. 'Your mother and I enjoy a glass of wine at night but your bold ... theft ... and your ... total inebriation ...'

'Terrible,' my mother added.

'A whole weekend wasted on a hangover.' My father shook his head. 'You are so immature. We'd thought with the new school ...'

What were they talking about? Wine? Theft? It took a moment for me to realise that my folks assumed my unconsciousness was caused by a gallon of cask wine. As if I would try to kill myself with Riesling! I shook my head in amusement and snorted like an incredulous horse.

'Don't you dare snort like that. What do you have to say for yourself?' Mum growled.

I wanted to say, 'Not guilty of being over the limit but guilty of attempted self-murder.' But instead I said, 'I'm sorry. I was stressed. It won't happen again. I've just been feeling very ... empty.'

Both parents stopped raging and looked at me.

'What could you possibly be stressed about? You have it all. We do everything we can to give you the best life possible.' Dad shook his head and slammed a plate of toast on the table. I knew it was true. 'We've sent you to ballet, to swimming lessons, speech and drama classes, piano. We've opened up so many opportunities for you. What more can we do to make you happy?'

Mum sighed in frustration. I gave a wak smile and a little shrug.

'Guitar lessons, maybe?'

Part 2.

WELCOME TO THE JUNGLE

11.

Embrace your inner rock star. It became my mantra. My dress sense was still more masculine than feminine but now I opted for a bigger and bolder version of my pirate persona with black tights, puffy shirts, shoulder pads and big, big hair. The fringed miniskirt and limbo-low cleavage look was not for me. Ankle boots and a dark slash of lipstick completed the ensemble.

My theatrical background meant I was comfortable on stage and although I shied away from singing in school musicals, rock singing was a whole different kettle of mullet. I was up for it. Madonna was no Dame Sutherland and frankly I'd listen to the Material Girl over caterwauling opera any day. I adored Madonna – the attitude, the irreverent Catholicism and the overt, uncontainable sexuality. Rejecting the dogma of my Catholic education, I retained a penchant for religious iconolatry: jewel-encrusted crucifixes appealed on a deep level. But what I loved most about Madonna was the gap between her front teeth.

My new look was a cross between Madonna and Kate Bush. Kate was built like me – thin with melonous breasts – although when I tried to recreate her haunting screech I sounded more like a dying rodent. We had studied *Wuthering Heights* at school the previous year and I'd fallen deeply for Heathcliff. Dark and brooding, he had much in common with my Poet – or maybe I just imagined the Poet that way. My own selfish rebellion was mirrored in Catherine's wilfulness. Sadly, it seemed our future together would be just as ill-fated as theirs, but nowhere near as interesting.

I'd owned a guitar since I was fifteen but it sat gathering dust and cockroach droppings most of the time. Occasionally I'd pull it out of my wardrobe and pluck the strings, trying to produce a melody. Now, with the pocket money I'd saved by abstaining from midnight romps, I bought a basic 'how-to' book of simple chords and progressions. Mum and Dad promised to send me along for guitar lessons if I spent a fortnight doing atonement for my alleged binge-drinking session.

With diligence and sombre patience I studied, minded my little brother and sister, washed up, hung out the laundry and cleaned the pool without complaint. I was a model daughter. I rang Bob, the former Skyhooks guitarist, and booked a weekly private lesson to start the first Wednesday after my two-week penance was up. This dangling carrot kept me on task for the two long weeks. My deep grey mood began to lift with the promise of rock stardom just around the corner.

Bob was a funny fellow, not what I had expected at all. Nothing about him screamed hedonistic rock star; he was more like a quiet guru, with an ethereally arrogant quality that was hard to define. Little wiry Bob, with his shiny head, tiny spectacles and aura of serenity, reminded me of Mahatma Gandhi, whom I had embraced as a hero after seeing the famous film the year before. Gandhi taught that anyone can hear the whispering voice within, if only they are ready to listen. Given the cacophony in my own brain – the constant bickering and shrieking and wailing and complaining – this message moved me profoundly. And it was a great relief to realise that my disappointment in Christianity was not unique. Gandhi said that while he admired Jesus Christ, he could not embrace modern Christianity because its adherents were so un-Christlike. I couldn't have said it better.

Bob lived in a converted garage in the shabby beachside suburb of Miami, under a house belonging to the parents of two drop-dead gorgeous young men who were playing in a new band with Bob. I met them once as they cruised through the garage during my lesson. My jaw ached at their physical beauty, but I put my cravings on the shelf and focused on my C scales. With years of piano lessons under my belt I had a basic understanding of musical theory. This helped, but only a little. My hands were small and I struggled to master some of the chords. To win a smile of approval from Sensei Bob, I would practise until I had blisters on my fingers. The professionals made it look so easy; Bob's fingers glided over the neck of the guitar like a skater on ice. I was about four steps ahead of a kindergarten kid with a recorder. I sounded awful.

Bob was a patient and talented teacher, although I managed to divert at least half of every lesson into conversation. While my guitar playing progressed slowly and discordantly, he kept me amused with rock and roll anecdotes, sprinkled with philosophy. He was perhaps the first adult male I had had such an opportunity to connect with on a platonic level – the big brother I never had. To him, of course, I was just another spotty kid without talent, but he never made me feel that way.

While Bob was a worthy mentor, his wasn't really the image I was going for. He could fine-tune my ear for music, but I needed a female role model. In earnest I began poring over magazines, searching for stories about female rockers.

Blondie's Debbie Harry was like a Barbie doll that had been left out in the rain, pretty in a post-punk way. But there was nothing blonde about me; I was the antithesis of a Barbie doll.

Pat Benatar was wonderfully angst-ridden. Her fuzzy Muppet hairdo and intense eyes were more my style. She was short with boobs and, in her tights and puffy shirts, looked like she shared my taste in fashion. But she was just so serious.

Madonna, of course, was the newest sensation. But it would be sacrilegious to blatantly copy her and anyway, I was no dancer. I would sing. I would rock. But I would gyrate, not dance. I would learn the guitar and maybe wield it occasionally, like Suzie Quatro or Joan Jett, but my plan was to be a killer frontwoman. I wasn't a great vocalist – but that didn't stop most rock singers.

A new girl had just burst onto the Australian music scene like a howling banshee: Chrissie Amphlett of the Divinyls. Straightaway I put my other heroes aside and Chrissie, with her unique guttural voice and slutty school uniform, became my idol. I clipped out photos of her and teased my fringe into a thick ball over my forehead. I practised my pout and kohled my eyes. She was so dangerous and brazen. I wanted to *be* her.

I studied my chords and warbled out tunes in my bedroom when no-one was home to hear me, all the while picking Bob's brains for inside information about the rock industry, filing away everything he told me for future reference. One thing all the women rockers seemed to have in spades was attitude. They reeked of anger and menace. Maybe it was just an act, a necessary protection in a male-dominated world. But female rockers were *tough*, and I was not. I was a giggling groupie, the silly plaything of rock stars. If I wanted to be a real rocker, I had to stop being used by them and stop using them. I had to learn to kick butt for myself. Snarling and pouting and frowning at everything, I rustled up some attitude, working as hard on my new persona as on my fingering.

The walls came tumbling down when Mum collected me from my guitar lesson one afternoon, a few months after my first session. Usually Dad parked on the street and read a book until I was finished, but Mum drove right up the driveway. The lesson ran a little over time and Mum glared as I farewelled Bob at the door. A gentle soul, Bob put his arm around me for a playful hug as I left. He waved and grinned as we pulled out of the driveway. He had such a beautiful smile.

Mum's silence told me drama was brewing.

'You seem very chummy with your teacher,' she spoke through tightly clenched jaws.

'He's really nice,' I offered tentatively.

'I think there's something not right about it all. He's bald!' she exploded.

'So?' I countered. 'Lots of men are bald. No big deal.'

'Old men. Men who have lost their hair are bald. Not young punks who shave it off as some kind of statement.'

'Mum, he's not a punk. It's just a fashion thing ...'

'It's not natural,' she fumed.

I couldn't help it. I rarely spoke back to my mother but she had it coming.

'Neither is your hair. You dye it blonde.'

I thought she was going to lose control of the car.

'That subversive attitude just cost you your guitar lessons. Over. Kaput!'

A wall of silence fell. Inside I was bubbling over with rage. In ways that I could not articulate, the lessons had been the therapy I needed to get me through my suicidal fog. I marvelled, at seventeen, at some parents' inability to nurture their children. Adults seemed better equipped to raise a pot-plant than a child. Sunshine. Water. Air. Soil. Easy. Children were more complicated, but not much – they simply needed enough space to be heard, to be safe, to feel and express their emotions, to make their own mistakes and to be loved unconditionally – whatever their musical tastes, their hairstyles or their clothes.

My parents provided a comfortable home. They encouraged and supported me in my studies and in a plethora of extracurricular activities. They worried about my spiritual growth and sheltered me from what they considered to be harmful influences. Almost everything in my domestic environment was designed to protect me – but nothing and no-one could protect me from myself. Without more candour between us, how could my parents know what it was that I needed, and what I needed protection from? Not even I knew.

I felt completely powerless. My opinions counted for naught and my status as a child meant I was unable to make important decisions for myself. In some cultures I would have been married, raising children and making decisions as a mature woman by seventeen. It was only natural that I would try to test the limits of the role society prescribed for me.

12.

In the privacy of my darkened bedroom, I continued to practise my guitar. I would draw the heavy gold curtains, sit on my green patchwork quilt, switch on my ghetto blaster and strum along, trying to wrap complementary chords around the melodies. Sometimes I'd put the tortured verse from my diary to music, creating odd reworkings of songs.

'The gold and emerald spider takes advantage of my pain. His eager eyes, they hypnotise and drive me insane. When I'm low and all is dark, he glows and aims his sting. That spider's poison eats my mind, though I try to hide beneath his wings.'

My songs didn't sound too bad when I was singing them. But when I recorded my masterworks to cassette and played them back, I knew I had a long way to go before anyone would pay money for such noise.

My sexual fantasies still revolved heavily around my rock and roll adventures, but after a few months off the horse, I was out of practice. It was time to get back in the saddle. I dutifully paid Sister Superior three dollars and snuck out for a tame night at a Pseudo Echo gig at Bombay Rock. I ended up backstage chatting to their lead singer, Brian, and bass guitarist, Pierre. I liked Pierre, but the attraction was purely cerebral. He was a walking hairdo and an interesting musician and we chatted about current affairs. This was a breath of fresh air in an industry that often viewed girls backstage as meat on legs. With their synthesisers and bouffant hair I considered Pseudo Echo a bit 'wet', but they were a decent bunch of young men. I made bedroom eyes across the room at their tour manager but wandered home in a wholesome state, proud that I could keep my knickers on if I chose to. The idea that I was addicted to sex had crossed my mind and I worried that it was like alcoholism or a poker-machine compulsion – something I needed to tackle.

Meanwhile, my 'real world' love life was cruising along in low gear. I had been dating Richard, a cadet journalist whom I knew through mutual school friends. We chatted on the phone and went to a few parties as a couple. The odd kiss goodnight in the front seat of his car when he dropped me home at a sensible hour; holding hands; not much more. I liked Richard. A good-looking young man with a wicked wit, he was the archetypal Nice Guy. I even started paying more attention to the morning newspaper, combing it for his articles. But I was not ready for a Nice Guy. I still had too many lessons to learn.

We hadn't seen each other for a few weeks when I heard from him one Friday afternoon. He'd been sailing the high seas in the Brisbane to Nouméa yacht race and had just come ashore.

'I'm going to a dinner at the Southport Yacht Club with the crew. Please come. I'd love your company. Really.' He was a smooth operator.

'I'll have to see. Mum mightn't let me,' I lied. 'I've got to learn my NIDA monologues.'

'Please cover for me, Mum,' I begged after hanging up. 'Tell me I can't go. I'll ring him back and say I'm not allowed to. I am just not in the mood to go to a sit-down dinner with a bunch of strangers. I have too much work to do.'

'Dickie is lovely,' my mother crooned. 'He's handsome and clever. Just go. You'll have a good time.' Protestations about homework and rehearsals would not sway her. I couldn't persuade her to ground me.

'I like Richard,' I moaned. 'I just don't want to marry him so there's no point pursuing it. Not this weekend.'

'Listen, love,' Mum urged. 'I was going out with someone else when I met your father.' She gave me a smile and a wink. My mother never winked. I shuddered.

Yachting was the sport of kings. Well, of the wealthy, at least. It was the gene pool Mum wanted me to be swimming in. And she would not take no for an answer.

Dressed in my green parachute pants suit and a dark scowl, I dragged my heels to the clubhouse on Main Beach. The stench of salt and seaweed hung in the air. A cool ocean breeze wafted back from the dunes. Richard and I joined a large table of rowdy crew. They were a mixed bunch, from young blokes with pierced ears and punkish hairdos to ancient mariners with ruddy faces and tubercular laughs.

Drinks flowed and the dinner was delicious. I loved food, and I relaxed and opened up in the convivial atmosphere. After the main course, the group decided to play musical chairs: every five minutes, every second person moved clockwise around the table in an attempt to get everyone more acquainted. I met such a lovely bunch of people, some shy, some gregarious. But when a Rod Stewart look-a-like sat beside me and gave me an enveloping smile, I melted. I wanted the table train to stop right there and then.

He sported spiked blond hair, an avant-garde outfit (with his pointed shoulder pads and crazy tie, he could have been a member of the Talking Heads) and a side-splitting sense of humour. We clicked like the final number in a combination lock.

'So you're still at school. A little schoolgirl,' he teased me.

'And what do you do then, ...?' I didn't even know his name.

'Billy. I'm Billy and I play bass guitar in a band.'

And there it was. The dial went click and the safe swung open to reveal the treasure inside.

I smiled at him with renewed interest. He did look like Rod Stewart. Tall – very tall – and lean. His smile was devilish and his blue eyes sparkled with raw energy.

When a sleeve of photographs from the yacht race circulated and I began dutifully to flick through them, my new friend began rolling his eyes and feigning embarrassment. I soon saw why when I got to the photo of him scaling a mast – completely naked.

'It was my twenty-first birthday,' he groaned. 'I was very, very pissed.'

I did my best not to peer too closely at the picture.

The night wore on and we were all invited back to the house of the owner of the yacht. From garbled conversations I gathered that not only had they not rated a place, they had gotten lost and returned to Brisbane over a week after all the other boats. Richard had a morning shift the following day and was keen to call it a night, but I gave him a pleading look and the poor fellow gave in.

We drove back to a lavish house in a waterfront estate. There was a sauna off the main bathroom. Decadence! It transpired that the yacht owner was the Rod Stewart look-alike's father and although Pseudo-Rod had a mousey girlfriend in tow, he showed me a flirtatious amount of attention, giving me a tour and plying me with alcohol.

Weird jazz oozed from the stereo and middle-aged drunks swooned about the living room, doing some kind of interpretive dance. When one of them pulled out a joint and passed it around, my eyes nearly popped out of my skull. I was pretty sure this wasn't what my mother had had in mind. I had a deep toke and fell instantly into a dreamlike haze. It was strong ganja.

Richard declined a smoke and sat in a corner like a guard dog, ears pricked for any sign of trouble. Pseudo-Rod looked deep into my eyes and told me his short life story. I heard only the words 'bass player' and 'punk band'.

He wanted me. I could see it in his steely blue eyes. His wallflower girlfriend sat like a bookend at the far end of the couch. Fate. Destiny. My mother had told me to come.

Much later, as my head began to clear, I wandered into the kitchen for a glass of water and saw again the photos of the failed yacht adventure. Furtively I shuffled through them and found a nice one of Pseud-Rob (with his clothes on). I tucked it into my parachute pants and hopped back out just in time for Richard's last call for a lift home. The gathering had melted into a wet smudge on the floor and I reluctantly said my thankyous and farewells.

Richard drove me home in silence and didn't offer me his smooth cheek for a goodnight peck. His disapproval hovered like a toxic gas between us. That was our last date.

13.

As the end of the year approached, the mounting pressure of final exams and the NIDA audition began to compete for my attention. When it came time to apply for tertiary places, my parents insisted I fill my wish list with teacher's colleges. They assumed I would become a drama teacher – but if NIDA offered me a place, they would not stand in my way. Even they understood the prestige it would confer.

The audition intake officer had warned me that I would be unlikely to secure a place straight out of school. Thousands of auditions were held all over Australia to fill the coveted forty places, which were usually awarded to more mature actors with some life experience behind them. Unperturbed, I recited my monologues in front of the mirror and resolved to give the performance of my short life. A spot at NIDA was a golden ticket for Aussie actors. Mel Gibson. Steve Bisley. Judy Davis. I was determined to be next.

The auditions began one Saturday morning in October. Dad drove me to Brisbane and left me on a bleak corner in the heart of the city, where a gaggle of trendy folk clutched steaming takeaway coffees. A small placard reading 'NIDA HOPEFULS' was tacked crookedly above a warehouse door. My belly was alive with crawling creatures and my mouth was dry. Every word of my monologues had flown from my brain.

My confidence deflated further as I surveyed the vibrant, older, *very theatrical, darling* crowd. Some of the girls were

Hollywood gorgeous. There were some raving queens and a few plain Janes, intense, beatnik types who looked like mime might be their forte. Introductions were restrained: seething distrust held us all back. Feeling like a stupid yokel schoolgirl, I fought the desire to turn and run after Dad's car like a puppy with separation anxiety.

At last we were called inside and divided into groups. The warehouse was hollow and cold with high, security-wired windows and an expanse of well-worn timber floors. The assessors flashed predatory smiles, welcoming us into their dramatic slaughterhouse. Like cattle in leg warmers we shuffled in, trying to focus on the demands being barked at us.

The auditions consisted of an elimination process: two hundred or so hopefuls went in and over the course of the day we would be reduced to thirty, who would return the following morning for a second round. My childhood ballet classes came in handy in the dance set, when we had to follow a series of quick routines. Lots of uncoordinated Marlon Brando types looked close to tears as they fell about the place like drunken clowns. My memory recovered and I delivered Lady Macbeth without a hiccup, much to my relief.

Soon morning tea-time arrived and a list of names was read out. My name was not called. Those whose were filed into another room and a pair of heavy doors closed behind them; the rest of us exchanged nervous glances. A perky blonde, vaguely familiar from a television commercial, arrived to speak to us and I prepared myself for a let-down. But she grinned and gave us a victory salute.

'Congratulations, artistes. You are through to the afternoon callback. We'll break now and have some morning tea.'

There were hugs and high fives and I felt a blush of confidence colour my cheeks.

As the day proceeded the tasks became more and more gruelling. I enjoyed the improvisations and managed to survive the other culls until I found myself on the list of thirty callbacks for the next day. I flew into Dad's car flush with hope and promise. I felt sure my future as an actress was secure.

Sunday was masochistically wonderful. They tortured us with more song and dance routines. They ripped my Puck to pieces and forced me to perform the entire scene again without words. I must have done something right because I was still on my feet at the end of the day, facing the assessment panel.

The esteemed John Clarke and Nick Enright gave me ego-fattening praise before breaking the bad news. I was too young. It wasn't an absolute no. They said they'd need to look at the numbers before making their final decision, but they braced me for the possibility of rejection. But the decision would hinge on my age, not my talent. They validated me as an actress and I could have kissed them. In fact, I think I did. It was the most wonderful rejection I ever experienced.

That hurdle behind me, I was left with the more painful obstacle of my final exams. I didn't succumb to the pressure that threatened to engulf some of my friends; being able to bullshit on cue was an advantage. When the afternoon of our last exam finally arrived, the school simmered with tense excitement. After thirteen years we were getting nearer and nearer to the real world. The final call of 'pens down' sparked a howl of adolescent release.

I had done it. Somehow, between abortions, sex romps and drug experimentation, I had finished. Even better, my every cell told me I had done well. I was sure my folks would be thrilled with my results. My father, beaming, had given me permission to party, but insisted he would come and collect me from wherever I ended up; he didn't want some drunken hoon driving me home. I suppose he was entitled to be nervous. Southport High had just released a whole new class of hoons into an unsuspecting society.

We spilled out of the auditorium. Hugs and kisses. Textbook bonfires in the garbage bins. The mood was electric. I racked my brain for some way to celebrate. Most kids just got paralytically drunk. My theatre friend Berzerko was taking circus classes and had mastered the art of firebreathing, which he demonstrated by searing all the paintwork off a teacher's Volkswagen. But I wanted something more. I needed a celebration to remember. Six days later, fate threw an opportunity to me like a juicy bone to a hungry dog.

Our school formal was fairly tame. Speeches. Non-alcoholic toasts. Drunk teachers. Synthetic music. The official party ended at eleven o'clock, when we all climbed into taxis to Surfers. Our childhoods were coming to a close and we wanted to assault the sand and surf in a closing tribute. A few southern revellers made their way to our sunny playground but in 1983, local schoolies still ruled the Surfers dunes. We sat on the beach and drank cheap flagon wine from little plastic cups we had begged from McDonald's, the sand cool and gritty beneath our feet.

The next day, through a soggy head, I received a phone call from a boy I knew vaguely from amateur theatre. Who? What? It took me a few minutes to unravel his words. He was desperately trying to find a date for his own school formal after his volatile relationship with a St Hilda's girl had soured. Paul was an unremarkable boy with pale skin, pale hair and a pale personality. Polite to a fault and the perfect gentleman. Not qualities that got me excited. But he was a nice private-school boy and my mother, of course, urged me to accept the invitation. Hoping for a top-notch affair and with luck some good food, I told Paul I would be his date.

I had donned my green pants-suit for my own formal, shunning the regulation taffeta and tulle, but I needed to up the ante for a private-school shindig. A little black cocktail dress did the trick, paired with tiny black pumps with a low heel. Hair pulled up into a loose bun. Quite classy, I thought. Kind of Audrey Hepburn at the end of a long day.

Paul collected me in a sleek white limousine and pinned a purple orchid above my breast. We crawled through the glittering metropolis of downtown Surfers, sipping champagne. The formal was at Sea World, which sat perched on the Spit, arrogant with fame and popularity. Just a giant aquarium, really. We dined on unpronounceable delights against a backdrop of fishes, sharks and stingrays, and then a group of us climbed to the top of the shark tank. My fingers grazed a fin as it swam past and a thrill of adrenalin tickled me. The dark skin felt like a cross between sandpaper and cold leather. A girl who had arrived with her date by helicopter threw her corsage into the black water and some creature from the deep swished past and gobbled it up. We laughed until tears ran down our cheeks.

Paul and his friends had rented a motel room and we went back there for a few Sambuca and lemonades after the speeches. When the roof of my mouth began to taste like toffee – not as pleasant as it sounds – I thanked Paul for the evening before making my way on foot back to Surfers. It had been a nice enough night, but I could feel that old tingle of boredom, urging me to seek out greater adventures.

As I stumbled through the well-lit mall I caught sight of Kirsty, my Australian Crawl groupie mate. She was loitering outside a late-night coffee shop with a gaggle of beautiful people. Kirsty and I had forged a shallow friendship based solely on our backstage pursuits. We exchanged sordid stories like trading cards whenever we crossed paths at gigs. Standing there now with her sprayed-on clothes, tight perm, beaming smile and the promise of trouble in her eyes, she looked like my lifeline to a more interesting night. When she gave me a wave, I walked over.

She grabbed my arm and whispered in my ear, 'Are you ready to party? Guess where we're off to?'

I shrugged.

'There's room for one more. We're going to Brisbane.'

Brisbane. I hesitated. I'd have to find a way home. It wouldn't do to be stranded in the city. Mum and Dad would flip. But I'd finished school. I was only a couple of months off eighteen – almost officially adult. What could they do? Kids were expected to let loose at the end of the year.

'What's happening in Brisbane?'

She leaned in close.

'Duran Duran.' She gave me a nudge. 'I've wrangled an invite to the after-party.'

I could only imagine how she'd wrangled something like that.

'Count me in,' I grinned. Any amount of grounding was worth a chance to hang out with one of the most famous bands in the world. I'd suffer the consequences later. Life was just a party and parties weren't meant to last.

With Kirsty and four girls I'd never seen before I squeezed into the back of a Jaguar, settling into the soft leather seat and admiring the classy wooden inlay on the dashboard. A seatbelt was not forthcoming but I held on as tightly as I could. The man in the driver's seat turned up the stereo and we shouted over the radio for the entire trip.

The other girls looked like friends of Hugh Hefner's and spent the next hour peering into impossibly small mirrors, applying lipstick and fiddling with false eyelashes. Tiny sequinned blouses were pulled open as the girls compared boob jobs. Condoms were passed around and intellectual critiques offered as to their various merits. These were seasoned vultures and they knew every trick in the book. The stench of exotic perfume hung in the air-conditioned atmosphere. Hair was bouffed and sprayed into masses of golden fairy floss and every female mouth but mine chewed on minty chewing gum. Give those jaws a work out, girls, I thought. You'll need it.

Our trip came to an abrupt end when we pulled into a very flash hotel in the heart of Brisbane. A hoard of screaming girls stood out the front. Apparently the band had just made their glittering return from the gig at Festival Hall. My sister Annie had attended the concert with her schoolmates, chaperoned by a group of mothers. The thought that hers might be one of the voices in the screaming throng thrilled me down to my neatly manicured toes.

The blonde cartel spilled out onto the footpath and the Jaguar disappeared into the night in search of a park. I was a good foot shorter than the stilettoed goddesses around me. In my sombre black dress and comparatively sensible shoes, my hair piled demurely onto my head, I could have been their parole officer.

Kirsty talked us through the security brigade in the foyer and we shuffled nervously into a lift. When the doors parted we fell into a party that snaked all the way down a hallway. The band had the entire floor to themselves and every room was full of revellers. Excitement hummed in the air. My pulse revved.

The crowd was not so different from the usual. There were plenty of familiar faces from the Gold Coast. But Duran Duran was the first supergroup launched by the revolutionary entity that was MTV. People had tried extra hard to look extra glamorous and were talking extra loudly, with histrionic head tosses and wild gesticulations. We were all showing off, vying for attention.

The vultures melted into the throng and I found myself alone and searching for a drink. I felt drab and depressing in my black dress; the other guests had embraced the spirit of Rio. Pushing through the crush of colour like a black widow, I came upon the welcome sight of a bucket of ice, the green neck of a champagne bottle emerging from it. As I searched for a glass, a voice beside me asked in a thick British accent, 'Are you after a drink, then?'

I looked up and did a double take. It was Simon Le Bon, one of the planet's most eligible men. Feeling like a terrified librarian, I nodded mutely, drinking in his smooth cheeks and full, pouting lips. He conjured up a glass, poured me some bubbly and, somewhat unnecessarily, introduced himself. I was captivated. I longed to stay glued to his side but we were soon joined by other hangers-on and, reluctantly, I moved back as the feeding frenzy consumed him.

The three Taylors of the band were being orbited by skimpily dressed satellites and the very androgynous Nick was holding court in his luxury suite at the end of the hallway. Like a visitor to an art gallery I wandered between the rooms, looking for a comfortable niche to settle into. Surrounded by hot-pink pumps and off-the-shoulder blouses, I felt unpleasantly conspicuous in this sea of glittering starfish.

Three or four champagnes later, I had taken my hair out, the bun leaving a nice wave. Like a heat-seeking missile, I had found my rock-star target and was in hot pursuit. Mr Leatherpants tantalised me with his chiselled cheekbones and feathered hair and honey-glaze accent. He was dressed in a three-quarter cream linen coat, skin-tight maroon leather pants that left little to the imagination and a puffy white pirate shirt. Furtive glances became knowing smiles and finally conversation. He was the archetypal rock god. Flashy and trashy, with all the confidence of a brightly burning star. He played with my hair and told me dirty jokes. His voice was divine and I was completely dazzled by this strange, exotic creature from the motherland.

I'd come a long way since my nervous debut with the Initiator. The shy schoolgirl was gone, replaced by a consummate huntress. Rock stars were fairly easy game and it was simple to reel one in if you used the right bait. I had learned fast that leopard-skin tights and spun-sugar hair might get you past the security guards, but more class than arse would get you between the sheets. Competition was intense and to win the rock star you had to be different. You had to stand out, one way or another.

This particular night, my black-widow garb worked in my favour. I looked sophisticated but innocent, unlike the mole patrol around us. The trick was to look and act like this was your first rock and roll party.

Leatherpants reminded me of a debauched Oscar Wilde. Pale and pretty, he seemed hyperactive and the reason became obvious when he offered me a line of cocaine.

'I've never done it before,' I confessed. Now I could be genuinely naïve.

He hooted with glee.

'Fabulous! A snow virgin. Allow me to introduce you.'

He tipped a tiny hill of white powder onto the glass coffee table. Suddenly partygoers swarmed around us, eager to be offered a snort. I'd seen plenty of cocaine before but I'd never had the courage to partake. People seemed happier and more talkative on it and I'd long since stopped believing all the horror stories we were told at school about drugs. A little upper here and a little smoko there didn't seem to pose too many problems; like guns, the real danger was in the user, not the instrument. Heroin scared me. I'd heard the rumours about some Australian musicians being junkies but I'd never seen it up close.

Leatherpants squealed as he bent down and chopped the powder into five long lines with a cardboard card. Pulling a plastic straw out of his jacket pocket, he offered me the first sniff.

Modelling what I'd witnessed at parties, I blocked one nostril with my finger and bent to the table with the straw to my other. I inhaled sharply and felt the coke hit my adenoids with a slap. A mildly unpleasant burning sensation travelled into my sinuses and an acrid taste arrived at the back of my mouth. Sitting back, my eyes watering, I waited while Leatherpants knocked back two lines in a snap and offered the other two to a heavyset fellow dressed in overalls – clearly one of the road crew.

The cocaine felt wonderful. I was sailing through a colourful dream like the figurehead on a runaway ship. Becoming bolder in my coquetry, I all but begged my rock star to bed me. I wanted to seal the deal before he was distracted by one of the lanky blonde wannabes.

I didn't need to worry. Leatherpants had hands like an octopus. When he kissed me, he tasted like a make-up palette. The man had more rouge and lipstick on his face than I did. After a few lingering wet kisses, he dragged me by the hand to the bathroom. We opened the door to find a man seated on the closed toilet with a woman's head bobbing up and down in his lap. Another girl was snorting coke from the marble bench top.

'Good work,' Leatherpants encouraged before shutting the door. 'Listen, love,' he whispered to me. 'I've got something for you and I am just about ready to take you on the bed, in front of the whole bloody circus.'

I was up for most things and I was throbbing for his affections, but sex in front of a roomful of people was not ever going to be on my agenda.

'Hang about,' he went on. 'Hey!' he called across the room to a rather weedy fellow in his early forties who was dressed in a crumpled suit. 'We need you.'

I frowned, hoping the wrinkled man was not going to be invited to join us.

'Come on, we're going for a drive.' My English rock prince kissed me on the forehead.

Ten minutes later, we were exploring each other's mouths in the back of a luxurious limousine. The chauffeur tried to keep his eyes on the road while I tugged at Leatherpants's pirate shirt, unwrapping my graduation present to myself. Leatherpants was all bones and his skin was deathly white. Without the fancy threads he seemed childlike and vulnerable. The strange thought struck me that this was someone's son. Not a god at all – just a boy, frail and breakable. I found the thought romantic. Pulling up for air and breathing heavily, I asked an inspired question.

'Hey, how about you drive me home? It's an hour away and we can cover a lot of ground in that time.'

Leatherpants poured two glasses of champagne and leaned forward to talk to the driver.

'Hey, man,' he growled. 'We're off to ...?' He raised an eyebrow at me.

'Surfers Paradise,' I called.

We knocked back the champagne and he tipped some between my breasts, licking it off while I struggled out of my little black dress. The idea that the chauffeur could hear everything and was possibly taking the odd peek in the rear-vision mirror I found very exciting. A whole roomful of people was one thing, but a solitary voyeur turned me on. I let myself be covered in kisses and lay back, my face pressed into the leather seat, as my new friend filled my blood with fire.

I had learned, in the previous two years, how to find my way around a rock star. They truly thought they were gods and it was important to worship. Preferably on your knees. Sweat glistened on my brow as we worked up a frenetic rhythm. Between shudders and sighs we did more cocaine and drank more champagne. The drug was a powerful aphrodisiac and I rode waves of ecstasy as a light rain began to fall against the tinted windows. Leatherpants pushed me and guided me to places I had never been and the pleasure was all the more intense with the thrill of being watched. I felt so very naughty.

He was an excellent lover, obviously well practised. He boasted of having bedded hundreds of women.

'Old. Young. Fat. Thin. Black. White. Four at a time!' he laughed.

'Well, practice makes perfect,' I giggled as I wiggled and bounced, shaking my hair and growling and howling like the proverbial hungry wolf. It was all about the performance, of course. An act. A vaudeville show. Rock stars liked theatrics. I looked down at this man who adorned the bedroom walls of girls all over the world. His eyes were spinning, his make-up was melting and he had the goofiest grin on his handsome face. This was what the Vulture Club was about. This was fun. This was as rock and roll as it got. All lingering sentimental thoughts of the Poet were blown out the window. I was hammering this rock god on behalf of every teenage girl who had rolled about in bed imagining doing exactly this – and it felt fantastic. The vulture had landed!

As we cruised down the Pacific Highway through the weary glitter of Surfers Paradise, I peeled my sticky, sweaty skin from the leather upholstery and gulped some more champagne before struggling awkwardly back into my dress.

'This is the life!' my lover said, raising his glass. 'Did I catch your name?'

'Nikki,' I laughed, knowing he'd forget it as soon as I was out of sight.

I warned him to tell the driver to turn left at the next set of lights and the limousine snaked down Monaco Street.

'Well ... thanks for that, love,' Leatherpants sighed, his trousers manacling his ankles together. He kissed me deeply before bidding me farewell as we pulled up outside my house.

'I'll be lonely now,' he pouted. 'I might have to sit up front and get the driver to play with my gearstick,' he laughed, pulling his clothes back over his skeleton.

'I can't imagine you'd ever be lonely,' I teased.

Looking up into his doe-like eyes as I climbed out of the car, I reconsidered. Maybe he did feel alone in his crazy world.

'Have a nice life,' I grinned, throwing the chauffeur a cheeky wink.

As the long car stalked back into the darkness, I shuffled into the house, my muscles already twanging with glorious pain, to find Mum awake with a cup of tea. It was four-thirty in the morning and she looked like she'd been crying.

'Did you have a nice time?' she asked flatly.

'I had a great time.' I smiled.

'That was very considerate of Paul to organise a lift home. Must have cost a bit. Was it nice in the back of the limousine?'

'Ohh ... it was very nice,' I said, licking my faintly bruised lips.

Mum had obviously peered through the front curtains and seen the car but not the date. I floated to bed, completely careless. School was over. I was set for Kelvin Grove Teacher's College and I had fulfilled my childhood fantasy to bed a fabulously famous, wealthy and gorgeous rock star. Life was definitely worth hanging around for.

14.

My celebrating done, the anticlimax hit me like a sledgehammer. Most of my friends were busy, away on holidays or drowning in family festivities. For a week I wallowed in domestic malaise. My littlest sister and brother, seven and five now, ran about me in manic circles. I played my guitar for them, making up nonsensical tunes about shark attacks. My chord progressions had come along nicely. Bob would have been proud.

Annie had started tweenie-dating and I teased her about her convent vow, asking for my hundred-dollar payout. All in good time, she promised. She was just assessing the alternatives first. We were getting along better as she inched into the world of boys. Her halo was slipping and it gave us something in common to laugh about. I knew she was thinking about my window-hopping and eyeing her own portal, which opened straight onto the front lawn.

Flicking through the newspaper for want of something better to do one morning, I stopped chewing my mouthful of toast and stared.

The Poet was back in town, performing at Bombay. One night only. My blood ran cold. I'd heard not a word from him – nothing since our briny encounter. The memories of the mess he'd helped me make prickled uncomfortably. I decided – masochistically, maybe – to go. If he didn't want to see me again, he could tell me to my face.

With six days to go, I began my campaign of beautification.

My plan was to look as goddess-like as possible. The Poet and his band were not into the 'dolly-bird' set. Blonde was crass and suntanned cleavages the pits. I needed to look dangerous.

I put a darker rinse through my mousey hair. *Cleo* informed me that a fruit and veggie detox would ensure a flat stomach, perfect skin and clear eyes within a week. My peepers looked all right already but my skin needed whatever help it could get. I had been plagued with spots, which I aggravated by picking, ever since puberty. I had taken to using concealer like putty filler and in summer my face melted like a messy Diane sauce. Now I gorged myself on apples, bananas, kiwi fruit and mangoes. My parents didn't stock a lot of vegetables; carrots and beans were the extent of it, so that was my dinner all week. Mum couldn't understand why I was turning down bangers and mash and roast chicken. Pimples, I explained.

Secretly I harboured a delusion that the Poet had lost my phone number and spent the last eight months pining for me, crying into his sauerkraut and schnapps for his lost Persephone. He was probably only doing a gig in Surfers Paradise to lure me out of hiding for a tender reunion, I mused. Delusions, delusions.

When my big night arrived, the truth was painfully clear. She was Nordic. Beautiful. A European study in perfection. And the Poet was head over heels, according to his bandmate, who chatted to me after the gig.

I'd seen her at the front of the stage during their lacklustre performance. Everyone had seen her. The woman was a model. A real model. Next to her I looked like a gypsy hobbit in mourning. The bandmate broke the news to me as gently as possible but warned me off heading backstage.

Speechless, disoriented, I wondered at my foolishness. The venue was emptying fast and I had no money for another drink, or for the fare home. Optimistic brand-new underpants had left me cash-strapped. I had assured my parents I was meeting up with friends and begged Dad not to collect me. I leant against a wall, took a deep breath and evaluated my options. Watching the road crew disassemble the amps and mikes on stage was like watching ghouls dissect my dreams. But then somebody behind me called my name. For a millisecond I thought it was *him* – but when I span around, I gasped. The last film I'd seen at the cinema was *An Officer and a Gentleman* ... Oohhh, my God, what a sexy, romanced-off-your-feet flick that had been. And in that instant, it was real. Hollywood meets Bombay Rock. Walking toward me, with a blinding grin and the laughing confidence of a court jester, was my Rod Stewart look-alike. I had stuck the stolen photograph of him in the back of my diary and scribbled the word 'HUSBAND' underneath, and now here he was.

He seized me by the shoulders. 'What are you doing here?'

'I was ... watching the band ... breaking up with someone ... you know, just another night. Where's your girlfriend?' I regretted the question as soon as it dribbled from my lips.

'Who cares? Let's go back to my place.'

I frowned curiously, happily. Did I look that easy? Was it my cleavage, my slash of dark lipstick or the glint in my eye?

'Sure,' I laughed.

We caught a cab home to the house with the sauna. What seduced me most about Rod – Billy, I mean – was that he was so incredibly funny. A born comedian on long, long legs. He had sun-bronzed hair spiked into what was later referred to as a mullet, sharp blue eyes and an Etruscan nose, all atop a tall, brown body, toned by professional windsurfing. Like giggling mice we crept into his bedroom and enjoyed one another. I had more scintillating conversation, more laughter and more sex in one night than I had had with any one male in my life. We lay awake and talked until the early hours of the morning. We were fascinated by one another. So many men have so little to say. Silent, muscled bodies. Billy was the opposite. There was a connection that transcended the physical. As sure as I was that the sun would rise, I was sure that I was going to marry Billy.

He was almost four years my senior and was something of a larrikin. He'd left school in year ten, which would horrify my schoolteacher parents. He had an earring – another black mark. And he had spent a few years playing bass guitar for a small-time three-piece punk band called the Wormz. Three strikes.

On my way to school I had often walked past a redbrick wall with the words 'The Wormz Are Coming' graffitied in huge letters. Billy told me they did a rad version of the Monkees' 'I'm a Believer' and promised to play me a tape some time. They'd supported the Sunnyboys and Jimmy and the Boys, a Sydney punk outfit notorious for their outrageous stage antics, led by the shockmeister Ignatius Jones. Jimmy and the Boys were unlike any other act in the country. Jones was supported on keyboards by the outrageous Joylene Thornbird Hairmouth, an over-the-top drag queen, and the band was infamous for staging violent shows. I'd seen them live and they were something else; they were one band I was never going backstage to visit! They had only recently disbanded.

'What were they like?' I asked Billy.

'Lovely. Really lovely chaps. Apart from the blood and the obscenities and the dismembered baby dolls ... they were really very nice.'

Billy's crazy tales of backstage escapades fascinated me and, inspired, I volunteered a few of my own adventures. He was as star-struck as I was and I felt no need to censor. The Wormz had dissolved when the drummer was decapitated during an ill-fated drive up Mount Tamborine.

We were so comfortable together. Some people are so guarded that complete intimacy is impossible, but Billy was the most open book I'd ever read and I felt safe being honest with him. In almost every part of my life, I hid behind masks of my own making. To my parents, I presented a conservative, studious, polite if rebellious young virgin. To my friends I was a wild, slightly insane tangle of hormones. To lovers I was a willing nymphet with few inhibitions and not a Catholic bone in my body. With Billy I was all and none of those things. I was myself.

Who was I, really? A sad and uncertain young woman who had been looking for affection in all the wrong places. My self-esteem was a parched and damaged thing, a crack running below the surface. I sensed a similar crevasse beneath Billy's cocky charm. We both felt underappreciated by the world and dreamed of fame and fortune, believing our talents would be better recognised in a big city. Fools or visionaries? Probably a little of both.

Billy's girlfriend was an obstacle. Technically they were still dating, although he'd recently moved out of their shared unit and back in with his parents. He walked me the three kilometres home as the sun began to crawl over the horizon and swore he would sever their threadbare romantic ties that very day. They'd been together for years and he dreaded the encounter, but he knew he would be setting her free to find someone more compatible. They were chalk and cheese, he assured me.

To say I spent the day in a state of nervous paralysis would be an understatement. Cruel voices taunted me, telling me that Billy would realise his mistake and run back into the arms of his girlfriend. Why would he throw away a relationship of so many years for a girl he'd known for a matter of hours? But my guardian angel countered, whispering that magic had occurred and that an army of angels would move heaven and earth to align us. It had been my blind date with destiny. All would be well.

At eight o'clock that night, Billy rang to tell me it was a fait accompli. And so our courtship began in earnest.

Summer loving. Our affair smelled of salt and tasted spicy. Almost every night we walked or taxied to Billy's parents' yacht. We made love in the forward cabin, the gentle motion of the water accompanying us. Afterwards, soaked in brackish sweat, we would lie on the deck and sample his father's wine. Billy loved the fine things: good wine, good pot and good sex. He was bored with his job as a windsurfing instructor and wanted to do more with his life. He'd finished more than half of a shipwright's apprenticeship before giving it away and was now considering going back to it. His older brother was an engineer, his sister a radiographer and his younger brother a champion windsurfer. Billy felt like the black sheep of the family and was itching to prove them all wrong. Without ever saying it outright, both of us felt that our futures, as far as the eye could see, would be shared. Like ham and pineapple on a pizza, we belonged together.

My letter of acceptance into Kelvin Grove Teacher's College arrived in due course, prompting much parental celebration and no enthusiasm on my part. The campus was in Brisbane, an hour away from home and from Billy, and it was not yet clear where I would live. The options, as my parents saw it, were boarding with a family in town or renting a unit with a 'suitable' flatmate. Needless to say, a boy would not be considered suitable. We inspected a few places and met a nice fellow who was renting out a room in his house, but he was a single middle-aged man and was vetoed instantly. The most agreeable solution, my parents finally decreed, would be for me to catch the bus to Brisbane every day, a round trip of more than three and a half hours.

By the third day of orientation, I had my doubts. In drama class we pranced about, pretending to be pineapples or floating like clouds, but my thoughts were with Billy and my desire to be a real actress. Did Debra Winger or Meryl Streep get to where they were with such nonsense, I wondered. I dreamed of New York. Broadway. Off-Broadway. Bacon and eggs at Tiffany's. But I had no money. I was completely reliant on my folks for pocket money, most of which I spent bribing Annie.

I began to feel claustrophobic. Surfers Paradise was being invaded by pensioners, attracted by the lack of death duties in Queensland. People were flocking to my hometown to die – and I needed to get away to live. I needed a bigger town and Brisbane was not it. It wasn't called Australia's biggest country town for nothing.

One sultry Monday evening on his parents' yacht, Billy planted the seeds of an idea.

'My little brother just got two big pay cheques,' he smiled cunningly at me. 'They're made out to cash.'

'You're not suggesting ...?'

'Just one ... he's overseas and he'd give it to me if I asked. It's just a loan. We'll pay him back when we hit the big time.'

'How much?' I asked hesitantly.

'Eight hundred and something. It's enough to get us to Sydney and keep us going for a couple of weeks. We'll get jobs. You could set me down in any city in the world with nothing but the clothes on my back and I'd land on my feet. I'll take good care of you.'

'Sydney. It's a long way. My parents would kill me. They'd send the cops or private detectives or something to drag me back.' I was thrilled and terrified at the same time.

'They couldn't,' he said. 'You're only three weeks off turning eighteen. You're free, sweetheart, so let's fly away together. Start a whole new life.'

'Sydney.' The word tasted good in my mouth. I rolled it about and savoured it. When I looked into his eyes, they were wide with suspense.

'Let's do it,' I laughed. 'Let's be mad and just run away.'

We walked all the way home from the darkened marina in the rain. Holding hands and barefoot, we hatched our crazy plan. Billy would cash his brother's cheque and book two one-way economy train tickets to Sydney. We would recruit a friend with a car to drive us to the train station, just over the border at Murwillumbah. And I would go quietly insane in the meantime, sure that my parents would find out and our plans would be thwarted.

Friday night was our moment. With the soundtrack of *Mission Impossible* ringing in my ears, I summoned all my acting skills, despite the gnawing stagefright in my bowels. I told Mum that Billy and I were off to see Max Bygraves in Tweed Heads, warning her that it might be a late night. The choice of Max Bygraves was bizarre and inspired. He was an ancient crooner and comedian who held not one iota of appeal for me. But I knew Mum would be pleased that my tastes were 'maturing' and there could be no reason for her to withhold her permission. I had already smuggled an overnight bag to Billy, who had handed in his notice and taken the day off work. My bag contained three changes of clothes, my diary, make-up and some photos of the family.

Annie, of course, sensed that I was up to something. I caved in and confided in her, mainly because I wanted her to stick up for me once I'd gone.

'You're pregnant, aren't you?' was her first question.

'No! Really, I'm not. Make sure you tell them that tomorrow. I do love them, Annie, and I know this will make them angry, but I feel so trapped. I'm on their life path and I need to get off it.'

Annie promised not to breathe a word until the next day. I had written a long letter to Mum and Dad, asking for their understanding. I knew no words would make them feel how badly I craved independence, but my letter tried. I gave it to Annie and asked her to sneak out in the early, early morning and slip it into the morning newspaper. I gave her my alarm clock and begged her not to forget. She gave me her word.

Tears stung my cheeks as I said goodnight to my littlest brother and sister. I gave Mum a warmer farewell than usual, hoping she'd one day understand what I was doing. And as I rushed out the door to the waiting car, I gave Annie a tight hug, whispering a promise in her ear.

'I'll be rich and famous before you know it and you can come and have fabulous holidays with me.'

15.

With that wired, slightly nauseated feeling of having been awake all night, we stepped onto Platform One at Sydney's Central Station. The sounds of pigeons in the rafters and early morning traffic greeted us – a bored city welcome. Taxis lined the streets but we decided to head into town on foot, exploring the sights at ground level.

Heading north up George Street, I was fascinated by the grime and the colour of the capital city. Exhaust fumes filled my lungs. It was eight in the morning, the start of a busy working day, and a simmering expectancy filled the acrid air. Souvenir shops were hanging out their Jimi Hendrix and Che Guevara T-shirts and their tables of gaudy snow bubbles and velveteen wall hangings.

After a greasy breakfast of sausage rolls, we asked for directions to Kings Cross. Ignoring the homeless people sleeping on every street corner, we made the long, hot walk up William Street towards the red-light district. I harboured a seedy desire to live in the Cross. Maybe because it was one of the few suburbs I'd heard of; maybe because its tarnished reputation epitomised what we were hoping to encounter in the big city.

It was everything I had expected. A dirty, broken-down old hooker of a place. We inspected the cheapest bed-sits and one-bedroom units we could find, but the options were depressing in the extreme. Deciding to try further afield, we trekked up into Taylor Square and along Oxford Street, where we passed more openly gay men than I had ever seen before. I thought of my gender-testing school friends, Berzerko and Paul, and wondered what they were up to. I hadn't even told them I was leaving.

I'd spent a restless night on the train, half expecting the police or my parents to board at every stop. I'd done a complete sweep of the platform before alighting, paranoia perched like a neurotic goblin on my shoulder. Only Sam and Rhonda knew where I was and had sworn to reveal nothing under pain of death. As even I didn't know where I'd be staying, there was little they could share anyway. I wondered how my letter was being received back at home. Annie would be being interrogated at the dining-room table. Mum and Dad would be furious. Change is always uncomfortable, but progress requires it.

At Darlinghurst we sat down with a local paper and desperately searched the classifieds. The rents were exorbitant.

'We're going to have to get jobs and save a bit,' I pouted.

Billy nodded.

'Let's find somewhere to stay for a few days. A cheap motel or hostel or something.' He pointed to a bunch of ads on the next page for hostels in Bondi. Bondi Beach. Maybe the beach would be a nice place to begin our life in the big smoke. On foot, mindful of our limited finances, we walked all the way down Oxford Street.

Falling in love with Paddington and its sardine-packed terrace houses, we continued through the shopping metropolis of Bondi Junction and dragged our weary feet down Bondi Road until finally the glorious Pacific rose up before us. The famous curve of sand glistened with promise and a sign in a window offered rooms for twenty dollars a night. A big yellow building called the Thelellen Beach Inn, it was perched at the top of the esplanade like an art deco castle, with sweeping views over the beach. The price was right and our blistered feet could not go another step, so we checked in and let ourselves into a weathered but spacious room with two double beds, a small table and two chairs, a fridge and an electric kettle. The shared bathrooms were at the end of the hall.

Flopping down onto the orange terry-towelling bedspreads, we fell into a deep sleep and stayed that way until dusk, when the sound of screaming sirens broke our slumber. After enjoying our first romp as de facto man and wife, we headed into the buzz of Bondi. The vibe was casual but everybody seemed so beautiful and sophisticated. A hundred different tongues chattered, Japanese tourists and European backpackers and Middle-Eastern kebab spruikers all calling into the sea breeze. There were black people. I'd never really noticed, but the Gold Coast didn't seem to have any black people. Nearly all of the people in Surfers were gold.

That night, we laughed and drank red wine and shared our hopes for the future. We strolled along the beach, watching the festival of coloured lights winking along Campbell Parade. Before we could chase fame and fortune we needed a permanent roof over our heads and a source of income, but our first night in Sydney was for romance.

Day two was devoted to job hunting. We dressed in our best gear and headed into the city on a grimy bus. Both of us had full-time work before lunchtime. I was to start the next day in the kitchen of a funky vegetarian café and Billy was to sell jeans at General Pants. We were over the moon; we could feel providence looking out for us. With selfish joy I completely forgot about the life I had left behind. There was only forward.

I began squishing boiled eggs and mayonnaise between my fingers at eight the next morning. My co-workers were large, lesbian heroin addicts, which was kind of ironic in a health-food café. Despite their pinned pupils and the occasional 'accidental' body rub, they were lovely people and I enjoyed the work. It wasn't long before I noticed something else about the place: our clientele consisted primarily of musicians, including some minor celebrities.

'EMI recording studios are just around the corner,' my boss explained. Well, that made me love the job even more. Perhaps I could schmooze up some session work for my bass-playing boyfriend. Between the cheese grating and the onion slicing, unfortunately, there was little time for schmoozing.

Our first Saturday in Sydney was my eighteenth birthday. I opened my two presents, both from Billy: a hardcover book of pictures from Marilyn Monroe's last photo shoot and a little plastic Academy Award. We were having a night out to celebrate thanks to my guitar guru, Bob, who was living in Sydney now, playing with the Young Lions. They had a midnight gig in the Cross and Bob had promised to put our names on the door. We played dress-ups in anticipation, trying on all the clothes we owned in different combinations. Billy wore my red and black pin-striped jacket, a pair of skin-tight black jeans and (at my request) a little eyeliner. I opted for basic black and a pair of fishnet stockings I'd picked up in Bondi. Lots of make-up. I could have passed for a panda.

Kings Cross at night was like nothing I had ever imagined. We tried not to stare as we passed a pudgy prostitute, dressed only in tiny silver hotpants, sweat-stained bra and a cut-off white fur coat. She was tap-dancing on the pavement to a ghetto blaster blaring Shirley Temple, trying to attract trade.

We asked directions of a murderous looking biker and walked down a seedy back alley towards a narrow, well-lit doorway guarded by a human Rottweiler in a suit. Half expecting to be king-hit, I squeaked out our names and told him we were on the guest list. He checked his little black book and nodded us through into the inky darkness of the Manzil Room. My first Sydney gig.

The venue was one long corridor, dankly lit with a roof that barely cleared the top of Billy's mullet. Smoke filled the air and the crush at the bar was three or four deep. Where the Bombay Rock set was a rowdy mob of salty, sun-kissed surfers, the Kings Cross crowd was hardcore. Clothes were black. Hair was black or white-blond. Make-up was heavy, with deep dark eyes and vampiric lips. Girls favoured short skirts, cleavage and suggestive stances while the boys flashed hairy chests and tightly packaged pants. We braved the bar and ordered drinks before making our way to a safe spot just left and centre of the stage.

The Young Lions burst onto the stage like a cyclone. Those breathtakingly gorgeous brothers from Bob's house on the Gold Coast played the audience into a frenzy. Frontman Jeffrey's tight black leather pants air-fucked their way through the first set while his brother Clifford beat the life out of his drum-kit, showing off arms that looked good enough to lick. The music was loud and furious and the show was like a raw electricity cable, sending dangerous sparks in all directions. At half time the boys came out and said hello. We all caught some fresh air outside, shooting the breeze until it was time for them to be back on stage.

Halfway through the second set I began to feel like throwing up. My head throbbed and I broke out in a clammy sweat. Worried, Billy insisted we cab straight home. By the time we turned the light on in our room, I was bordering on delirious and stripping my clothes off to collapse on the bed. Within minutes I was up and running stark naked down the hallway to the bathrooms, where I threw up until my ribs felt they would burst through my flesh. Billy brought me a blanket, wrapped me in it and helped me back to bed. He sat with me all night, bathing my hot face and feeding me little sips of water.

The next day we did a post-mortem of the night before. I'd only had three drinks so wasn't stupidly drunk – but I'd left my drink on a table while watching the boys play. We concluded that someone must have slipped something into my glass. That or I'd picked up a bug. But Billy didn't get sick, and we'd shared an awful lot of bodily fluids in those first few weeks. It was a timely reminder to be on my toes – we were in the big city now.

16.

Surfers Paradise was fast becoming just a long, neon dream. On our very first day in Sydney, I'd sent my family a postcard, letting them know I'd arrived safely and telling them not to worry. Since then I had sent another couple and had spoken to Sam and Rhonda, both of whom had been subjected to a third-degree interrogation by my parents. Mum and Dad were convinced I must be pregnant, despite my friends' assurances to the contrary.

My life was filled with laughter and friendship and crazy dreams now, thanks to Billy. I was happy. But early one Sunday morning, as I sat on the grassy incline above the sand of Bondi, I watched a storm approach from out at sea. The sky was a menacing deep grey and the seagulls against it were luminescent. Other birds preyed on flapping cardboard pizza boxes in the car park. As the thunder began, I felt a rumble of homesickness. Guilt washed over me. My mother had cried, my friends had said. Tears filled my own eyes at the thought. I had worried only about her rage, ignoring the possibility that she might miss me, her eldest daughter, and be afraid for me.

She didn't know that I was more streetwise than she could imagine. And I could not explain to her how deep my need for Billy's love was, and how badly I had needed to leave. I went back to the lodge as soon as the first thick blobs of rain began to fall and wrote to her, fat teardrops staining the page.

After a few weeks of conscientious saving, we moved into an apartment in Sussex Street in the heart of the city. Our fifteenth-floor unit overlooked the clock tower at Town Hall and the newly built Sydney Entertainment Centre was not far away. We searched noticeboards and found another couple to share the rent with us. Glen and Cherie came from some sleepy outback town and, like us, had come to the big smoke with knapsacks full of dreams.

Within a week Billy and I were having second thoughts. Glen turned out to be suffering from debilitating depression or psychosis or some combination of the two. He was on medication but it didn't seem to be working. He refused to leave the house and Cherie was more of a psychiatric nurse to him than a girlfriend. She would paint the town red with us each weekend, but when we returned we took it in turns to go inside first, to check if Glen had hung himself while we were out. Billy and I began to go out every night just to get away from him.

One Friday afternoon at the end of March, after a long week at work, Billy and I sat at our laminex dining table as Glen began to cry, from his room, at the top of his lungs. We ate some cheese on toast for dinner but could barely hear each other over the din. Finally I'd had enough. I wanted to do something wild and amazing and most of all I wanted to get out of the apartment. A light-globe clicked on in my brain.

'Get dressed up,' I smiled at Billy. 'Get *really* dressed up.'

'Why? Where are we going?' he frowned.

'Elton John is on at the Entertainment Centre.'

'We haven't got tickets ... or any money. I just paid the electricity deposit.' He shrugged apologetically.

'We won't need money. Just get dressed. I've got a plan.'

Billy put on some fine threads and a little make-up. I dressed in a blue two-piece sequinned suit that I had found in a charity shop, donned a large feather hat and we were off.

'How are you going to pull this off?' Billy laughed as we walked the two blocks south to the large auditorium.

'I've got an idea,' I said in a patchy Scottish accent, throwing him a cheeky grin. 'You just keep your mouth shut and look pretty.'

'Whadyer mean, we can't come back?' I stood firm, glaring at the beefy security guard. This one had a gun on his hip. Heavy-metal security. Billy shuffled nervously behind me, keeping mute. I let fly another tirade in a thick Scottish brogue.

'Just tell Elton that Nicola Stewart is waiting to see him. He'll be annoyed that you're giving me a hard time.'

'Look, love,' the man smiled, showing me his ham-like hands. 'You're not on the list. There's nothing I can do about that. My hands are tied. I'm just doing my job.'

'Well, of course I'm not on the list, am I? I'm here to surprise the dear. Just be a good laddie and get someone to send a message to Elty. Just tell him Rod's little sister and her husband are waiting outside being hassled by security.' My accent was a mess, lilting from Scottish to Irish to a bastardised Russian, but I soldiered on, mustering all the cocky confidence I could.

'Rod Stewart, love. This is all so frustrating ... can't you just get someone to nip back and whisper in his ear?' I frowned. 'Surely you've got more big muscle-bound security cockies about. Come on ... the show'll start soon and I want to say aye before he goes on. For luck and all.' I gave my most doleful look, sweetening it with a flirtatious wink.

This went on for half an hour. More guards were called. They couldn't decide whether to believe me or to write me off as a complete nut job. No-one wanted to bother Elton. It could have meant their job. In the end I wore them down and the head of security nodded wearily for the doorman to let us past.

As we strode backstage, a surge of excitement ripped through me. The daily grind of work and bills and grocery shopping had settled into a necessary but vaguely unpleasant scum on the surface of my dreams. But going backstage to visit Elton John – a meteor had landed in our murky pond, dispersing all traces of surface sludge.

'That was amazing. I'm in shock,' whispered Billy.

'Just keep walking. Don't look back and we'll keep a low profile for a bit.' We burst through heavy doors into a darkened room full of people. Most lounged in comfortable chairs, enjoying champagne and gourmet nibbles. The grand master of the Australian music industry, Molly Meldrum, sat quietly by himself in a large armchair, watching an enormous screen. With his trademark Akubra and famous jowls, he looked faintly disoriented. As the host of *Countdown*, he had more power to make or break emerging artists than anyone in the country. More importantly, he was friends with Rod Stewart. I grabbed a champagne to quell my nerves and made a beeline for him.

'Hi, Molly,' I enthused, sitting down beside him.

He gave a distracted nod of acknowledgement.

I looked around for Elton but saw him nowhere. Suddenly the spectacled icon, dressed in typically flamboyant costume with his trademark glitzy glasses and oversized hat, burst onto the screen before us and the show began. Everybody watched in silence, quietly moving their hips to the beat.

'Who was the support act?' I leaned across and asked Molly, trying to make conversation.

'Um ... Mondo Rock ... Did you miss them?'

'Yeah.'

More silence.

As Elton hammered his piano, the comfortable punters backstage had the best seats in the place. Although it lacked the sweaty intensity of the front of house, there was an egotistical thrill just in being there. I watched in silence with Molly for a while, then wandered off to find Billy deep in conversation with Ross and Pat Wilson. Ross was a celebrated singer-songwriter and producer, having fronted Mondo Rock and, before my time, Daddy Cool. Pat, his wife, was at the time enjoying a brief burst of stardom with her candy-pop single 'Bop Girl'. Billy was regaling them with the tale of how we came to be backstage and they insisted I demonstrate my Scottish accent. Ross declared it the worst he'd ever heard.

All around the room, long trestle tables sheathed in white damask bore rows and rows of champagne. The French bubbles smelled sweeter than the cheap champers I was used to and I mingled gleefully, chattering my way through the throng before finally ending up back with Molly. I'd watched very little of Elton's performance, but I'd certainly seen a swankier side of the music scene.

Molly, meanwhile, was staring intently at the big screen. He seemed hypnotised. I made some more small talk but suddenly, in the middle of one of my half-formed sentences, he leapt to his feet and ran from the room like a jack rabbit. I wondered if I'd said something offensive. Embarrassed, I slid into the warm chair he'd left behind, took a sip from my crystal flute and focused my attention on Elton. To my great surprise, Molly appeared onstage and launched into a rather terrible duet of 'Crocodile Rock' with the superstar. Oops. I had almost made him miss his cue.

Elton appeared some time after his show had ended. He'd clearly been washed and dressed to meet his admiring posse. He wasn't as short as I'd expected. All that sitting at a piano had made me think of him as about three-foot tall. He had an amazing smile, mischievously contagious, that seemed to slice his face in two. As admirers milled about him, Billy came over and whispered in my ear. We'd been invited back to the Sebel, where Elton was staying, for a party. As we didn't have a car or taxi money, we decided to walk and left straightaway, knowing it would take us at least half an hour.

The hotel was in Kings Cross, down behind the El Alamein fountain. When we arrived – a little tipsy, Billy wearing my ridiculous feathered hat – the guests were already mingling around the bar and the foyer was full of people searching for a glimpse of Elton. There was much whispered conjecture about his recent controversial marriage to his sound engineer, Renate Blauel. Word on the street had long been that Elton was gay, and rumours circulating the Sebel had him tumbling with everyone from Molly Meldrum to David Bowie. Was he covering up his homosexuality with a sham marriage, doing some shifty business deal, or genuinely in love? A glimpse of the blushing bride would probably have been even more exciting than one of her husband, but there was no sign of her. Instead, the artist formerly known as Reggie Dwight, surrounded by an entourage of beefy blokes, cut a swathe through the crowd and disappeared into a lift, not to be seen again all evening.

Billy and I sat cross-legged on the floor with Ross Wilson and drank beer straight from the bottle. I didn't care much for beer, but Ross was an entertaining chap with a wicked sense of humour. At three in the morning, we stumbled home through the slumbering city to the sound of snoring from doorways, where human bundles of rags dozed away. On the way upstairs I grabbed a handful of letters from the mailbox without looking at them. Probably just bills. We kissed passionately all the way to our floor and quietly let ourselves into the apartment.

Glen was still crying in his room. His anguished howls came from some deep cavern of despair that no anti-depressant could light. Cherie had left a terse note on the coffee table, telling us she'd had enough. She was going back to her inbred town. She did not use the word inbred in her note.

This left Billy and me with a real dilemma. Cherie had paid the rent for both of them and Glen was completely incapacitated. We couldn't cover his share, but kicking him out presented a few problems. He wouldn't want to go. He had nowhere to go and probably not a cent to his name. He hadn't left the apartment since we'd moved in. We went to bed and I lay awake, alternating between reliving the party and worrying about what we would do. At some point it occurred to me that we could simply push Glen from the balcony and call it a suicide. Even he would probably think this was a good idea. Lonely and irritable, I woke Billy.

'I think we should drop Glen off the balcony,' I whispered.

'Fine,' he smiled, half asleep. 'First thing in the morning.'

By the sober morning light, of course, I'd discarded the idea and went into Glen's room to tell him he was being evicted. He was so soundly asleep that I couldn't wake him. His snoring made me despise him more than I thought possible. Shrugging and slamming his door behind me, I went to the kitchen and ate a bowl of Cornflakes, trying not to indulge in murderous fantasies.

I flicked through the mail that I'd left on the kitchen table the previous night. Bills, bills, bills ... and a letter from Rhonda.

I recognised her dramatic swirl and ripped it open excitedly. It was a card decorated with scarlet stilettos. Reading. Reading. Rhonda was in Sydney! She'd sent the letter on Wednesday and had been about to fly out of Brisbane that afternoon. It was now Saturday. She'd included a Sydney phone number and after a quick shower and change of clothes, I hurried downstairs and walked to Town Hall to find a public phone.

A man answered and passed me to a sleepy Rhonda, who growled, 'Hey, foxy lady.' We chatted for a bit – she was very impressed with my Elton John tale – and agreed to meet up.

'I'm in Paddington, staying at this funky house,' she enthused. 'The guys who live here are great ... so much fun. Why don't you come over?' She was suddenly wide awake. 'And hey, just out of interest – they've got a room they're trying to rent for ninety bucks a week. It's a great room. Would you guys be interested?'

17.

From the bus stop at the Five Ways roundabout in Paddington, Billy and I walked down the gently sloping footpath of Goodhope Street. The suburb was steeped in history, and after the shiny tinsel of Surfers the tiny wrought-iron gates, quaint courtyards and ornate terraces made me feel I had stepped into an earlier era. I was certainly dressed for one, my puffy white pirate shirt billowing from beneath a thick black belt. Rouge slashed my cheeks in stark stripes and my hair was teased into a frizzy halo. Billy was a worthy partner in his stove-pipe jeans, green-and-black striped shirt and dangerously pointed shoes. We looked like we'd just jumped Black Beard's ship.

For years, 39 Goodhope Street had been dubbed 'Boystown'. A slightly shabby double-storey terrace painted faded yellow, it was the colour of a piece of newspaper left in a bottom drawer for twenty years. Skeletal trees and shrubs stood guard in the neglected excuse for a front courtyard. Thick black bars lined the front windows, as if the house was afraid the convicts might escape. A heavy wooden door with an ancient brass doorknob opened to Rhonda's blazing smile.

'Welcome, people.' She dragged us down the tunnelled hallway to the living room.

I had never been inside a terrace house and was fascinated by the long, narrow layout. With framed gold records on the walls and faded green velvet lounges, the house was homely and hip at the same time. We were introduced to the two current tenants, Joey and Jock. I wasn't sure which was Rhonda's latest squeeze but soon discovered it was a fairly interchangeable arrangement. Jock was a tall but wiry fellow who could have given me a few tips on my Scottish accent. About thirty, he was charming and talked a lot about his work as a sound technician for Midnight Oil. Joey, a little younger, did lights for the Divinyls and was a small, ferrety guy with dark eyes and a floppy fringe. He busied himself in the little kitchen at the back of the house, making coffee and cracking open a packet of stale lamingtons. In what might have been a dining alcove sat a strange contraption that looked like a torture device.

'I hang upside down,' Joey explained to me. 'For my spine.'

Upon closer inspection, I found that a giant pair of shoes, like snow boots, encased a person's feet while they were elevated in mid-air. It was a hanging-upside-down machine and possibly the strangest thing I had ever seen.

'That can't be very comfortable.'

'It's actually very peaceful,' smiled Joey as he bit into a coconut-encrusted cake. 'You should try it.'

We were shown the large master bedroom upstairs, where a cute balcony overlooked the barren front courtyard. It was a beautifully furnished room with a large bed and an antique dresser. A lovely, intricately detailed mirror hung on one wall.

'It's great,' I whispered to Billy, who nodded in assent.

'We've never had a girl live here. It's been strictly boys' own. But hey, it might be nice to have a den mother,' Jock laughed.

'Plenty of girls visit but none get to stay, is that it?' Rhonda teased.

With that, we all sat down and did the paperwork and made it official. I would be the first woman to live in Boystown. I felt quite honoured. In a neat twist, our room had just been vacated by Shane, the roadie who had let me backstage at my very first Australian Crawl gig at Bombay Rock. Boystown had a long rock-and-roll history and was inhabited by a changing parade of roadies, techies and musicians. The tenant backlist included members of the Divinyls, Hoodoo Gurus, the Models and the Angels and crew members from just about every band that had ever appeared on *Countdown* or in *Rolling Stone*. All watched over by Possum, the house cat, so named for her enormously bushy tail. She was a beautiful tabby with the most gentle and affectionate nature. I loved her immediately.

'She just leapt through those bars on the front window one night,' Joey told me. 'Straight into my lap.'

We raced home and packed. As our apartment had come furnished, we only had the bags we'd arrived with. Glen was still soundly asleep and we left our keys on the table and crept out quietly. No note. No confrontation. Stuff the lease, bugger the rent and screw the flatmate from hell. Later we'd wonder how long it took Glen to realise that everyone had abandoned ship and left him floating in his own little apartment in the sky. We couldn't help but laugh. Cruel but funny.

We moved into Boystown just as Rhonda flew back to sunny Queensland, and so began our roller-coaster ride into rock-and-roll Disneyland. Life would never be the same.

Flatting with Jock and Joey meant never having to pay to see a gig ever again. We were suddenly on the door-list for just about any act we wanted to see. In the first few months we watched Midnight

Oil turn the Hordern Pavilion into a fiery cataclysm, the Divinyls tear into an audience with ferocious energy, the Hooters bore an auditorium to death, Paul Young whine about where he'd left his hat and INXS seduce their fans with sultry grunt.

Billy and I were in our element, and we became quite arrogant about our newfound status. I'd been promoted from groupie to friend of the band. No longer was I hooking up with musicians in tawdry motels; I was travelling to gigs with them and shooting the breeze during sound-check. This was a whole new side of the game.

We also became quite snobbish in our attitude to the punters. We watched most gigs from the side of the stage, so as not to be contaminated by the plebeian masses out front. This was particularly true of bands like Midnight Oil and the Angels, who had quite blue-collar followings. The singlet and flannelette-shirt brigade would get drunk and spit and fight. We were above all that now; we were with the band.

At Pseudo Echo concerts we'd laugh at the cockatoo hairdos and lose sight of our own ludicrous reflections. We didn't want to be boxed into one particular category. We weren't mods, or heavy-metal boofheads, or new-wave romantic knob-jobs. We were serious pub-rockers, into real music. At home around the Boystown dinner table, we'd argue about bands like our parents argued about politics. Groupies, roadies, techies and us – we were all fiercely loyal to the bands we supported.

The music scene was changing, with new styles and sects emerging. There were still a few Sid Vicious characters lurking about the edges, but they were morphing into a more gothic type, epitomised by Nick Cave and his dark-lord cronies, crooning about suicide. Deep down, however, I remained a pop tart and avoided this more serious stuff. I liked songs about safe topics – love and sex and the wider world, things outside of me. I didn't want to listen to music that made me look too hard within. I feared I might not like what I found.

In the months since I'd left the family home, my domestic skills had gone into hibernation. I revelled in mess and loved the freedom of living in chaos. Joey put an end to that. He was a lunatic when it came to housekeeping. Many a time I was woken by him slamming the vacuum cleaner against my closed bedroom door at three in the morning, having arrived home from a gig and found the place dusty. He raged through mountains of dirty crockery, smashing dishes as he went. His ranting and hyperventilating became tiresome after a time, and so I pulled on the rubber gloves and got into the swing of being more house-proud.

Billy taught me how to cook. His spaghetti Bolognese ran rings around my parents' dry and crumbly mince-based meals. Rich tomatoes, crunchy celery and carrots, a huge crush of garlic and fresh basil were topped with shavings of parmesan cheese. It had never occurred to me, growing up at home, to take an interest in the kitchen and at work I did little more than grate cheese and squish boiled eggs. But Billy had a recipe book full of interesting dishes in his head. Having imparted his culinary wisdom, he promptly resigned any interest in actually cooking again and I became the stereotypical little wife, doing all the cooking for the household. The boys loved it and for a time I was happy to inhabit this old-fashioned fantasy. But when a pizza parlour opened up the road at Five Ways, I gladly hung up my wooden spoon and we returned to eating takeaway nearly every night.

When we could afford it, that is.

Money was tight. Growing up with two parents who worked meant I'd never experienced anything remotely like poverty. I had never wanted for anything as a young girl, but now I found myself living in the big city, trying to scratch together enough to pay for an endless stream of bills, not to mention drinks and clothes and food. I started slipping occasional apples and bananas into my bag at work, just to tide us over until payday.

Billy had given up his job at the clothing store and was getting the odd bit of freelance work from the shipyards down at Rushcutters Bay. These jobs were infrequent, but the money wasn't half bad. I was still working in the café, slaving over boiled eggs and lentil burgers and wondering what the hell this had to do with my dreams of fame and fortune. Between work and gigs and partying, when was I supposed to forge a career as an actress? I lay awake at night, listening to Billy snoring, and scrunched the sheets into balls beneath my fists. Oscar. Hollywood. New York. Yet I was wafting through my days as a frazzled kitchen-hand.

'What happened to you becoming a rock star and me becoming a film actress?' I asked Billy one morning, watching shards of sunlight stab his freckled chest.

'It takes time. Hey, but I saw an ad on a noticeboard for a bass player ...'

'That's bullshit. We have to start doing something real. With all our contacts, can't you get some session work?'

'I don't see you auditioning for anything.'

'We had all these dreams, and now we're just pissing them away, partying all the time.'

I sounded like a drag but it was true. We were getting nowhere.

But maybe our luck was about to change. One night over a few drinks, Billy told Joey he'd had some training as a boat builder.

'So you're handy with a hammer, are you?' Joey looked interested.

'Mate, I could build you anything you want. What do you want, a boat, a table, a book case, a house?'

Joey leaned across the table. 'A stage.'

And so Billy's new career as a rock-and-roll stage designer began.

Meanwhile, I quit my job at the café and decided to hit the talent agencies. It was time to kick-start the career I had run away from home to pursue. Billy had been given a generous advance for his first set – a design of his own invention for an upcoming Divinyls tour – and I was anxious to get some real work as an actress. Somewhat ironically, my dad provided what proved to be my first real break.

Buoyed by our new living arrangements and my happiness with life in general, I had finally found the courage to phone home and chat with my family. Huge swells of emotion washed over me when I heard my parents' voices for the first time in months. They cried and I cried. There were no recriminations, just joy that we were speaking again. My siblings sent me funny little letters and drawings and I felt closer to them all than I ever had before, now that I was no longer secretly wrestling against my parents' discipline.

During one of these phone calls, Dad told me excitedly about a new Australian film he had invested money in. *Bliss*. It was being adapted from the Peter Carey novel and was currently in pre-production, Dad explained. He urged me to seek out the casting people and try for a role. I took his advice and made some calls, finally learning that Suzie Maizels was the casting director. She had offices in North Sydney and so, without warning her, I put on my best outfit, did my hair nicely and caught the train across the Harbour Bridge. I would just rock up and charm her into casting me in the film, I reasoned. Naïveté can sometimes be an asset.

'I want a role in *Bliss*,' I announced as she emerged from her office into the waiting room.

'I'm sorry, dear, that's already been cast. Who's your agent?'

I shook my head and shrugged. 'I don't have an agent. Are you sure there isn't a small role ... anything? I am a very good actress. Really.'

'I'm sure you are,' she smirked. 'Get yourself an agent and some photos and we'll talk again down the track.'

'What about something in another film? I'd even do television.' My voice was firm and I was not moving. She put her hands on her hips and narrowed her eyes thoughtfully.

'You know what? Can you come back tomorrow at, say, ten o'clock?'

I nodded enthusiastically.

'There's something about you. I think you'd be good for the role of Lucy ... we haven't signed Gia yet.'

'Gia Carides?' I asked.

'Yes,' Suzie said. 'Do you know her?'

'Not personally,' I smiled sweetly. 'But I believe she has lovely teeth.'

The next day I was standing in front of Peter Carey, who sat in a bean bag, and Ray Lawrence, the film's director. After a casual conversation and a reading from the script, Ray asked me to meet him in the city the next day for a screen test. I was so puffed up with hope I thought I might burst. Halfway home I rang Billy from a public phone because I couldn't wait to tell him the news.

Life was moving in the right direction; I could feel the cold gold of Oscar in my little hands already. I had three pages of script folded up in my pocket and a copy of the novel, lent to me by Peter Carey himself. I stayed up all night and read it from cover to cover, with Possum keeping me company by licking my feet. *Bliss* was the most bent and beautiful book I'd ever read.

I was to read for the disturbing role of Lucy Joy, who gave her brother blowjobs in exchange for drugs. She was sassy, ruthless and perverse, all beneath a demure facade. She was me all over.

The screen test was an ordeal and a half. I was paired with Alex, a young actor who took the whole thing very seriously. Knowing we were both novices, Ray gave us all he could to get our best performances.

'Nikki,' he chided me. 'You are obviously a good actress, but you're coming across as a stage actress. There are three kinds of acting. Theatre, television and screen.'

He turned the television screen around and replayed us the scene we'd just done. I cringed. On camera my acting came across as melodramatic. I was over-acting, and Alex was doing the same. We were trying too hard.

'The camera picks up everything,' Ray explained. 'On a stage you need to act. For film you need to *not* act. Let the script carry the story. Act inside. Words and eyes. That's all we need. If you try hard to let your face do nothing, no facial contorting, almost no expression, the performance becomes real ...'

I tried the next take the way he suggested and the result was infinitely better. In all my years of drama classes and in the countless years as a struggling actress that still lay ahead of me, Ray's would remain the best advice I was ever given. I got a call back. Sadly, Alex did not.

The following week Ray asked me to test with Miles Buchanan. With cushions for lips and angelic curls, Miles had the demeanour of a middle-aged man but looked about twelve years old. In fact he was the same age as me. We were given three scenes to work on before another series of screen tests and I caught the bus up along the northern beaches to his family home to rehearse. Acting with him was a joy and I was more than a little impressed by the Logie he had won as a child five years earlier. The Logie was a distant cousin of Oscar, after all.

Despite Ray's encouragement, Suzie Maizels rang me at home a couple of weeks later. Peter Carey had decided to go with the actress with film experience – Gia 'sparkly teeth' Carides. I couldn't help but wonder if my chompers had anything to do with his final decision. But I was pleased to learn that Miles had scored the role of Gia's brother. Out of anger and childish spite, I didn't buy or read another Peter Carey novel for years. A year later, I managed to score two tickets to the première of *Bliss*; Dad sent me his complimentaries. I don't think he ever saw a cent of return, so it was a fizzer all round for us.

18.

I was by no means ready to give up on Oscar – but I familiarised myself with social security and began rocking up to their disillusioning establishment fortnightly with an unemployment form. Shoving my disappointment behind me, I threw myself into partying. Paddington was like a village, abuzz with social opportunities. Around the corner lived Pinky, a tiny English lady in her late twenties with a shock of short white hair and a belt of rock-star notches that left mine for dead. She was pretty in a damaged sort of way, like a parrot who'd been caught in a storm. According to her, no Australian band that had toured Sydney was free of the taint of her love. She was my first female Sydney friend and became an honorary Vulture Club member. With ten more years' experience than I had, she thrilled me with her sordid stories.

Not far away in Boundary Street was another house of rotating rockers, and Michael Hutchence had a pad nearby in the creatively named Paddington Street. It was common enough to start a party in one house and crawl through the suburb from venue to venue, nearly always ending up in the Manzil Room. A seedy but convivial dive, the Manzil was the equivalent of our late-night lounge room, where big names stole away on their nights off to jam with local musicians. We saw members of George Thorogood's band, John Cougar Mellencamp's band and someone from Fleetwood Mac. When they jumped on stage at three in the morning they might find themselves playing alongside the guys from Cold Chisel or Rose Tattoo, or a kid from the Western suburbs with a slide guitar. Cocaine and speed were the drugs of choice but anything and everything was available in the public restrooms. Every girl there was a current, former or future groupie or rock star.

Chrissie Amphlett, the school-uniformed strumpet who fronted the Divinlys, threatened me with a cat fight one night after finding me sitting in a booth with her boyfriend. He was raving about her while I pitched my idea for a new band, inviting him to back me. I have only vague, swirling memories of her wide-eyed rage and Pinky's laughter as she took bets on the outcome of our scrag rumble.

I woke up the next morning at home in Paddington with a swollen top lip and no recollection of how I'd got there. An interrogation of Billy elicited nothing but a knowing smirk. Had I come off the worse, or had Chrissie? Perhaps I'd just passed out on the table and hurt myself. I never knew, and Chrissie was nice as pie the next time I saw her. Whatever happened in the Manzil Room was swept out the front door and taken away with the garbage. Every night was a chance to start again. For those who suffered from chemically induced blackouts, this was a godsend.

The Manzil might have been our collective lounge room, but there was no shortage of late-night venues in the Cross. After hanging around with the boys from Pseudo Echo one night, we all traipsed back to a bar called Benny's. Billy and I had heard of this legendary place and had even tried to gain entry one night after a gig, but this was no ordinary nightspot. Located in Challis Avenue in Potts Point at the northern end of Kings Cross, it was open only to those who made the grade. The grade was 'fame'. If the doorman recognised you from *Countdown* or *Neighbours*, you were warmly welcomed. If you were a kid wanting autographs, you were politely told that the place was full.

A nondescript building hidden behind a big wooden door with a fish-eye spy hole, the place was a rabbit warren of three rooms over two levels, separated by three small staircases of five or six steps each. A fourth room directly left of the front foyer served as the bar. We'd been shooed away on previous occasions, but this time, being with the band, we were ushered in with smiles and pats on the back. Almost immediately I bumped into James Reyne, who bought me a drink and then returned to his gaggle of girls.

The place was dim but not as murky as the Manzil Room. There were some very dark corners but the bar area was relatively well lit. It didn't start really buzzing until well after midnight, when musicians would start arriving to relax with a drink and plenty of cocaine. Rock memorabilia festooned the walls and a little kitchen out the back could throw together rice or sushi for anyone whose appetite hadn't been dulled by drugs.

We took our drinks and sat around a big round table on the uppermost level. Glenn Shorrock of the Little River Band and his wife, Jo, squeezed in next to me and we made small talk. Jon Farriss of INXS tapped his drumsticks on the table next to ours and gave me a nod of acknowledgement, our paths having crossed during my Surfers Paradise heyday. It was a little odd to find myself in cramped quarters with Billy and a cast of characters from my lusty past – but this was the music world, where promiscuity was the order of the day. Lines of coke were passed around by friendly faces, to be snorted discreetly behind the laminated wine lists.

There was plenty of posing and preening going on and I'm sure egos collided more than occasionally. That first night, we watched Brian Mannix from the Uncanny X-Men pushing his bantam-sized weight around, preening like a peacock in his fashionably slashed singlet. He was hilarious, a pantomime unto himself with his pouts and head tosses. The stereotypical rock star.

The staff of Benny's was made up of Mickey, her dark hair pulled back into a severe ponytail, Molly, a mischievous, hard-rocking Shirley Temple who looked like she'd won a fight or two in her time, and Dominic, an elfin Frenchman with long hair trailing down his back behind an inexorably receding hairline. We soon discovered that the staff were the backbone of Benny's, as highly revered as the rock stars they served. No-one gave them any sort of attitude and if they'd tried, Grant and Marty, the Kiwi brothers who owned the place, would have had words. Benny's would go down in Australian rock history; it was the coolest place to drink in Australia in the eighties. Three lines of coke and four vodkas and orange later, I had decided that this was my new local. If I was ever going to rub shoulders with Rod Stewart, this was the place where it might happen.

After hours of basking in rock celebrity, a group of us bundled into the street and, laughing loudly, wandered through the jaded twinkle of Kings Cross as a pale purple glow consumed the sky. We made our way down a little alleyway off Macleay Street and dragged ourselves up a staircase to Baron's, a seedy, inviting bar with chunky, worn leather couches. The cocaine supply had dried up for the evening, so alcohol would have to do. Some patrons even drank tea. The idea of going home to bed was distasteful.

The actor Jack Thompson was banging something on the piano and I wandered over, sat on the stool beside him and played him my faulty, halting version of 'The Baby Elephant Walk'. It wasn't Hollywood but it was a world away from Surfers.

By the time Billy and I fell into a cab, it was broad daylight and my eyes were screaming for a pair of sunglasses.

For the next couple of months we fell into the same routine at least three or four nights a week: a rock gig followed by the Manzil, Benny's and Baron's. We usually took Mondays and Tuesdays off, lazing on the couch, drinking and watching *The Young Ones*, which we taped from the television. If the boys were on tour, we would sneak into Joey's room and fumble around under his futon for his collection of porn videos. We spent many a lazy afternoon eating hot chips and laughing at the incredible feats of some overweight Greek man who cheered 'Bravo' with each climax. We usually ended up acting out some of the scenes, but generally more for comic than erotic relief.

Most days featured drinks and a smoke with Pinky and whichever musicians and technicians were passing through. When Joey and Jock were away we'd host short-term housemates, rock and rollers who spent days asleep and nights on the town. The roadies were all known by cryptic nicknames: Junior, Head, Pineapple, Bat, Spider, another Spider and Sneaky. Sometimes I felt like Snow White! Our mailbox was always full of postcards from exotic locations and I began a lifelong collection. Billy and I had the place largely to ourselves during these spells, which was a lovely domestic arrangement – most of the time.

Although we were a tight unit, envied by many for our obvious devotion to one another, tiny cracks were starting to show. Nothing catastrophic – but there were moments of darkness, black spots on Billy's charming, boisterous exterior. For weeks he had worked like a man possessed on his stage, labouring over a revolutionary steel-grilled set of his own design. The structure filled the dining room like a menacing metal spiderweb. But now the Divinyls tour was about to get underway and he was behind schedule. He sat around for days on end, eating kippers and tomato sauce out of a tin. The fish repulsed me and his loss of motivation scared me.

'Get up and finish the stage or you'll be letting Joey down,' I whined one afternoon.

'I'm just feeling flat. Stop hassling me. You're turning into a nagging old shrew,' he mumbled into his fishy can.

'Get up and do some work!' I yelled, hands on hips, shaking with frustration. 'We're behind in rent and Jock is hassling me. Please.'

'Why don't you go out and get a job, then? I don't think I want to do this stage thing anymore.' He threw me a sideways look and a smirk, like he was fishing for a reaction. He always got one. Away from my parents, I was suddenly very adept at expressing my anger. I grabbed his can of oily kippers and dumped them over his head and then stared, waiting for him to say something. He looked like Carrie with rivulets of orange liquid oozing over his face, pooling in the corners of his mouth and dribbling down his white T-shirt. A minute passed in suspended animation before he darted out his tongue and licked a flake of kipper.

'Hmmm. Yum,' he murmured and we fell into each other's arms, laughing hysterically. Possum turned up to feast on the crumbs of fish that were dropping to the floor from Billy's head.

'Shit,' I said, looking down at the stained carpet. 'Joey's gonna kill us.'

In the end, Billy pulled himself out of his slump in time to put the last frantic touches on his stage. The finished product was impressive and Joey was pleased he'd taken Billy on. We'd expected Billy to join the Divinyls on tour, helping to assemble his masterwork at each new venue, and we'd saved our pennies in anticipation, even avoiding the cocaine lure of Benny's. But at the last minute the tour manager reneged; it would be cheaper, he decided, for one of the regular roadies to put the thing together. Poor Billy was devastated. Only he knew how to assemble the stage correctly. They'd screw it up and he'd never work again, he cried into his Bourbon. But Joey kept us in the loop, ringing us from around Australia with updates. The stage was a hit and Billy was soon lined up for more work with Midnight Oil and Spy vs Spy. Commissions began pouring in and soon he was hardly ever home, instead spending long hours at a rented warehouse, knocking out stage after stage.

More out of boredom than anything else, I found a job in an exclusive children's wear store on Oxford Street. Located in an awkward spot between Paddington and Darlinghurst, it had very little passing trade and some days not a single customer darkened the threshold. I spent my days behind the counter reading novels, rediscovering this neglected passion of my childhood.

As jobs go it was idyllic, but it didn't last long. My employment was terminated when the establishment closed down, having seen barely ten customers in a month. I couldn't have cared less. Life continued in a haze of gigs and parties.

We were dirt poor. My clothes were always a tad musky. The hairspray helped to conceal it, but the underlying stench of badly laundromatted clothes was ever present. I felt physically run-down from all the partying, with mouth ulcers, the occasional sty in my eye and a permanent hangover. Our fabulous lifestyle was starting to smell mouldy, and it was getting harder and harder to be loyal to my dreams. Oscar was getting tarnished. He was beginning to look like fool's gold.

19.

Late in June of 1984, I received a disturbing phone call. Guy McDonough, the guitarist for Australian Crawl, had died of complications from pneumonia. I sat in our lounge room, frozen to the spot, listening to rain drum down on the roof and the distant buzzing of an anonymous electrical appliance. Lighting a cigarette and inhaling deeply, I let the tears roll down my cheeks. Guy was twenty-eight. It was the eighties. I couldn't understand how a young man could succumb to something like pneumonia. Surely hospitals were equipped to fix things like that. Like all of us, Guy might have indulged in some risky behaviour – but he was a gentle soul. I could not believe he was dead.

Remembering our roof-top conversation years before, and the musical duet we'd played in my parents' lounge room, I put on an Australian Crawl album, cracked open a bottle of cheap champagne and raised a glass. An incredulous hush descended over the music industry for a few days. Guy was buried in Melbourne and then life went on. Live now, pay later – it would take more than one mishap to make us question that motto.

Months passed, and gigs began to blur into one long fuzzy din. The late nights left me with puffy red eyes and a bad taste in my mouth, while boredom left me on edge. I was becoming cranky. Intolerant. Homesick. Our friends were fun and good for a laugh, but there was a competitive, bitchy undercurrent to these friendships. Our social life was inseparable from the drug scene and it was all beginning to feel rather shallow. I found myself ringing home more often, just to hear the voices of people who loved me.

Late in the year, as the first warm sea breezes hit the air after a dry spring, I was home alone and woke at my usual time: midday. There was no bread in the house and I was completely addicted to soft white bread. Billy told me it would be the death of me.

'You'll blow up into a soggy white mass and die. That stuff is bad for you,' he'd lecture.

It was hard not to laugh at this advice, coming as it did from a man who enthusiastically smoked, drank and snorted whatever was on offer. I banged and crashed my way through the kitchen cupboards and bent down to peer into the mouldy fridge, to no avail. The mould was a clue that Joey was overseas.

The humidity was already spilling into the house, bathing me in a layer of sweat. Dressing in a light summer dress, with no bra or knickers, I found the keys and unlocked the deadlocked front door. As I closed the front gate, I bent to give Possum a tummy-tickle. She was sprawled out on the hot sidewalk like a bearskin rug. Purring, she rolled her legs into the air and gave a long stretch, before licking the skin of my hand with her sandpaper tongue.

'I'll bring you some tuna, Poss,' I smiled, giving her another scratch.

Wandering up Goodhope Street to the local deli, I took in the terrace houses, which continued to fascinate me. A mansion across the road still had its old carriage house, with a driveway running through to what were once the stables. The walk was a steady uphill climb and I was puffing just a little when I noticed two punks approaching from the opposite direction. They were hardcore, their faces full of metal and their hair spiked up about their heads as high and sharp as bayonets. I smiled nervously, but their close-set eyes and surly expressions did not invite friendliness. As we passed each other, one leered and called in a gravelly accent, 'Nice tits, bitch!' I frowned and hurried on, cursing them very quietly under my breath.

The corner deli was expensive and upmarket and we rarely frequented it. I found a small can of tuna, grabbed the softest loaf of bread I could find, paid at the counter and re-emerged into the glaring sun. Squinting, I made the easier trip downhill, unwrapping the bread and tearing into the soft, white dough with my teeth.

As I neared home, I could see Possum up against the wrought-iron fence. Something about the way she was lying chilled me to the bone and I broke into a run. When I reached her, I could see immediately that she was dead. Her neck was at an odd angle from her body and as I gently rolled her over, I saw that her eyes were glassy. She was warm and soft and a wad of pain caught in my throat. Coughing and reeling, wanting to scream, I stumbled to the front door.

Inside, shaking, I raced to the phone. Joey would know what to do. I ran my fingers over the tour sheet beside the phone and found that he was in Texas. A twangy receptionist answered and I asked to be put through to Joey's room. I had no idea whether it was 2 a.m or 10 in the morning.

'Joey speaking,' came his chronically chirpy voice.

'It's me. Possum's dead,' I blurted out. I was too upset to sugarcoat it.

'What?' A gasp. A pause. And then, in a softer voice, 'Was it a car?'

'No, I don't think so. There were these punks walking down the street. Real arsehole ones. I think they killed her. Her neck's broken but she's nowhere near the road. She's near the gate and she never goes in the street.'

'Calm down. Look, I'm just racing out to a gig ... I'm meeting the band for dinner. I'm just as upset as you are, but what can I do? You'll have to bury her in the backyard. Maybe she was hit by a car and the person stopped and put her on the footpath.'

'It was those bastards,' I fumed as the tears began to spurt. I sobbed and sniffled into the phone.

'Put a blanket over her, honey, and wait till Billy gets home. Or call Pinky. I've got to go.'

Joey hung up and I blubbered into my hands for a while before taking some deep breaths. I couldn't leave Possum out on the pavement. It was undignified to have people looking at her or dogs sniffing at her. I got a blanket, gently wrapped her up like a little baby, and brought her cooling body inside. I sat on the couch and rocked her in my arms, singing softly as tears dropped onto her lifeless whiskers.

When Billy arrived home, he dug a hole in the backyard. We buried her and said some special words to send her off to cat heaven.

Being faced with death got me thinking about life. It got me thinking about my life. I felt like someone who had been following a false map. All that rags-to-riches garbage, all those Cinderella dreams sold to impressionable young girls. I'd fallen for it hook, line and sinker. Run away to the big city with a handsome musician. The spangle of fame is just around the corner.

I wished I had a friend I could confide in. Someone who would understand my fears and frustrations. A friend who would challenge me to be the best I could be. Billy was just too busy and I could feel the shadows falling between us. We were always surrounded by people – at home, at gigs, wherever we were – and yet I had never felt so lonely.

I determined to start looking for work as an actress. After all, that had been my prime motivation for moving to Sydney. If I wanted that Oscar and a brownstone mansion in New York, I would need to pick up the pace. I wanted to go home in a blaze of glory. Perhaps a ride down Cavill Avenue on a float, holding my Oscar aloft. 'Gold Coast Girl Makes Good.' I wanted my parents to be proud of me and love me for who I was, not for what they wanted me to be.

I needed an agent; I needed work. But fame and fortune, I knew, were still a little way off – and a part of me knew I couldn't wait that long to see my family. I would find an agent. I would get work. But first, I needed to go home.

Part 3.

RECKLESS

20.

The train trip from Central Station to Murwillimbah was long and smoky. A fourteen-hour festival of nicotine and vodka. Billy and I had smuggled a bottle on board and had opted for the smoking carriage, which proved to be a mistake. A compartment full of people all puffing away like they were involved in some tribal smoking ritual, non-stop for hours and hours, is like being trapped in a noxious sauna. Smoking was a habit I'd picked up again after the move to the big smoke. That train trip cured me of it. Almost.

The north-coast township of Murwillumbah was steamy and lush. Mt Warning hovered behind it like an ancient gate-keeper, a relic of a volcano from eons ago. My dad and I had almost climbed to the very top some years earlier. Dad had always been a great lover of nature and I had a trove of happy memories of long bush walks in the Gold Coast hinterland.

Dad collected us at the station, tearful with joy. His chin quivered and he held me tighter than he ever had. He gave Billy a friendly handshake and seemed positively thrilled to see us. All my terror and apprehension about our reunion melted. My fears that I would be kidnapped back or chastised mercilessly appeared to have been baseless. At home, Mum held my hands and rubbed them, her eyes wet and her nervousness as palpable as my own.

After a loud and lovely reunion, my poor mother was most uncomfortable about where to accommodate Billy and me. Not wanting to endorse sin, she finally decided we could sleep in the same room – my little brother David's room – but in twin beds. David would sleep on a foldout bed in Rachel's room, which had once been my room. It was strange to be home again and I spent some time sitting in my old room before bed, remembering my teenage craziness.

My little brother and sisters had all grown up so much. That saddened me a little, and their innocent joy at having their biggest sister home filled me with guilt. Sister Annie by now had a steady boyfriend, but her opportunities for mischief were narrower than mine had been: she whispered that Mum and Dad had put security screens on the windows after I left.

I could see, reflected in my parents' eyes, the observation that a year had changed us too. Billy and I looked paler, thinner and a little strung out. Mum's dinner was probably the first well-rounded meal we'd had in months.

I tucked Rachel and David into bed and closed their door. I called out 'Night, Mum. Night, Dad.' And it felt nice.

Andy Gibb, still in orange overalls and his ludicrous buck-toothed smile, now sat on Annie's bed. 'I'll always have a soft spot for you, Andy,' I whispered, blowing him a goodnight kiss.

We also stayed with Billy's parents for a few days. They were much more relaxed than my family, probably because Billy was the third of four kids. We swam in their pool, drank their wine and were entertained by Billy's dad, who'd once had aspirations of being a concert pianist. He played so eloquently I almost cried. Late at night, I'd tinkle the ivories of their sleek black grand piano. My 'Baby Elephant Walk' sounded better than ever, but I'd forgotten how to play anything else.

All of my old friends had spread out about the globe. Tammy was at university in Armidale. Rhonda had gone overseas for a stint. I couldn't find anyone else but I didn't try very hard. I'd had a gutful of friends and I wanted to bunker down with blood relatives. I'd adopted Billy's family as my own and felt unconditionally accepted by them. This meant a lot to me, especially given my own parents' warier welcome of Billy. I could hear the undercurrent of disapproval when they asked about his schooling and see that Mum's eyes kept creeping to his opal earring.

The day of our departure, Mum took me aside.

'Why did you do it, Nikki? Was it something we did wrong?' Her eyes were full of pain and I winced, struggling to find the right words.

'It wasn't you or Dad. Really, I love you. But ...' my voice trailed away. I put my arms around her and we held each other, both with tears trickling silently down our cheeks.

'I miss you,' I smiled at her.

'I miss you too,' she smiled back.

On the train back to Sydney I cried for the first few hours of the journey, softly, silently to myself, while Billy slept. How does the gulf between parents and teenagers grow so deep? The bonds that were forged at birth seem to strain and fray during adolescence. It was like breaking out of the egg, I decided. The shell is going to get broken and the struggle might be painful, but if you stay inside because you're too afraid to leave or because the mother duck doesn't want to let you out, you'll die.

21.

We arrived home to the news that my old guitar tutor, Bob, had joined the Angels, a legendary tribe of hard rockers with some classic tunes. This was a great break for him, and we agreed we'd go along to their next gig to congratulate him.

Selina's at the Coogee Bay Hotel sat perched on the esplanade of Coogee Beach like a glittering gargoyle ready to pounce. The venue had a reputation as a rough place; fights tended to erupt nightly and sometimes made newspaper headlines. The crush of punters was decked out in blue singlets, flannel shirts and jeans, mostly young men with more beer and attitude in their bellies than was good for them. Westies, we'd have called them. We squeezed our way through the crowd to get a better view of the stage.

Bob played his guitar like a weapon and the Angels' frontman, Doc Neeson, had an awe-inspiring stage presence. When he wailed 'Am I Ever Gonna See Your Face Again?', the audience chanted back, 'No way, get fucked, fuck off!' with irresistible enthusiasm.

Afterwards, we caught up briefly with a sweaty Bob and promised to keep in touch. The band was touring relentlessly and his schedule had suddenly gone into overdrive.

I was happy for Bob. He was so very talented and unassuming. I, on the other hand, felt quite artless and crassly obsessed with celebrity. I wanted fame so badly it hurt and yet I couldn't wield a guitar or sing and the only professional audition I'd ever had, I'd failed. Hanging around famous rockers was beginning to highlight my own pointless obscurity. It felt a bit pathetic, in fact. I didn't want to settle for being a moth flitting about the light, occasionally getting burned. I wanted to find my own spotlight.

Bob was being cheered by hundreds of fans, but he was absorbed in his music and couldn't care less about the adulation. I wished I could have been so noble. I was beginning to suspect that fame was not something you earned or deserved but entirely accidental. Yet deep down in my shallow teenage belly, I still believed I was one of those accidents waiting to happen.

'Have fun,' I waved to him as we left.

'Go well,' he nodded back.

We soon settled back into our old routine, spending long hours at Benny's. As we lounged there one night, I found myself eavesdropping on the booth behind ours, where a man was talking loudly, doing whacky impersonations and throwing out ridiculous banter. I crawled up onto my knees and peered over the tall seat that separated us. Big brown eyes and nostrils stared back at me for a moment, then grinned.

'Dear God, it's an apparition!' he laughed.

'Hi,' I smiled back. 'It sounds like fun over there. Can we join you?'

'What's the password?' He winked.

'Mary, mother of God,' I retorted without missing a beat. A few drinks had loosened my brain and it was the first thing that came to mind.

'That's as good as any. Come on over. I'm Rhett and you are welcome in my court.'

'Your court?' I mocked, as Billy and I shuffled around to join his little posse. 'Who are you, the king?'

'No, my dear, I am the lord of all I survey.'

'A god, then?' I asked.

'Not a god, *the* God ... come down to earth as a man.'

'Well, that's a coincidence, because I'm the Virgin Mary.'

'You lie!' he shrieked. 'Mary, yes ... but not the Virgin Mary. You are Mary, the penitent whore.'

Billy looked flustered, unsure of what was transpiring.

'To Mary!' Rhett raised a glass to me.

'To ... the Lord, my God!' I responded, holding my drink aloft.

And so began my strange and bewildering acquaintance with Rhett. Billy was a key part of this friendship, and yet Rhett and I were so completely on the same wavelength – a strange frequency, and one which few could hear – that Billy often got quite jealous of our barely intelligible conversations, sure that there must be a subplot he was missing. He was wrong, of course – it was all just good-natured nonsense.

Despite my earlier resolve, my acting dreams were stagnating and I began to take my frustration out on Billy. He was spending his days in a valid pursuit. His stage sets were an outlet for his creativity and he was an extension of the bands he worked for. He was a notch or two up from being just *a friend of the band*. I resented that much more than was healthy and began to pick on him mercilessly.

When we met, I had been the rock chick, but now he was leaving me at home and living the dream – designing sets, jamming with the bands, joining them as an equal, not as a deranged fan. Meanwhile I wallowed through the days, dreaming of a career without doing anything about it. The turnstile of gigs and parties was draining. Nights were filled with the smoky haze of altered moods while the days were quiet and found me idle. I began to miss the old adrenalin rush of pursuing rock stars: aim, shoot and kill.

One night shortly after our return, I was walking down a staircase at Benny's when I bumped into a bloke walking upstairs with a drink. I looked up apologetically and drew a breath. It was Sex-on-Legs, a key player in some of my sordid fantasies. We knew each other a little, our paths having briefly crossed in the past. Only very brief introductions had ever transpired.

'Hello, there,' he said in a soft, velvety voice.

'Hi, I ... um ... sorry. I'll buy you another one.'

Looking down at my wet shirt, he smiled.

'Nah, it was only a soda. I don't drink.'

He took my hand and led me back to the bar.

'Mickey, pass us a towel will you?' he called to the woman behind the bar. In a sublimely sensual series of movements, he dabbed at my chest with the towel. My nipples startled under his touch and I blushed. He looked deeply into my eyes, then back down to my breasts.

'It's good to see you.'

He gave me a wink and a handshake and headed back up the stairs. Staring after him, I took a deep breath. I felt something I hadn't felt since I'd met Billy, and it frightened me.

Back on the other side of the bar with Billy and our friend Suzie, I stared as inconspicuously as possible at Sex-on-Legs, who was nibbling his girlfriend's ear. I burned with irrational jealousy. She was an attractive creature with long black hair and a wide smile. Not surprisingly, she looked like a model or a dancer.

'An exotic dancer,' Suzie whispered in my ear, catching my constant glances across the room.

Weeks went by and I couldn't shake those eyes and those fingers.

Given the nature of the Sydney music scene, I encountered Sex-on-Legs again before long. We danced a cryptic, sizzling dance, catching eyes, exchanging looks but avoiding any direct contact. Reluctantly, I appraised his woman. She was lithe and petite, but not awkwardly skinny like many muso-molls. Dark and mysterious with a body that was built for only one thing. Catching sight of myself in a full-length mirror one night at a party, I cringed at my frumpy presentation. My black tights revealed short but shapely legs, jutting out of impossibly sleek knee-high boots. But the pirate shirt made me look like Adam Ant's daggy little sister. Perhaps I needed to rethink the swashbuckling look and replace it with something slinkier.

I was sure I felt a spark between us, but could it all be in my head? The old tug-of-war between self-doubt and confidence began. 'You're imagining it,' a voice mocked whenever I let myself fantasise. 'He isn't interested in you. He just feels sorry for you.' But each time I saw him I felt lust boil in the saucepan of my belly.

Finally, one afternoon, he called Goodhope Street asking for Billy. Smooth. Billy wasn't home so I took the call.

'Hi. Ah ... hi. How are you?' I stammered, wondering how he'd found our number. Mind you, everyone probably had the number for Boystown.

'Great, love.' His voice was sweet and oddly courteous and sent tingles racing down my body. 'Hey, we're playing a gig tonight in the Cross. A little dive in Victoria Street. It's invitation only. No publicity. Thought you and Billy might like to come along.' He let the sentence hang for a lingering moment before exhaling, and I wanted to draw deeply, breathing him in over the phone like a cigarette.

'Yes. Sure. Yes, we'll be there. Thanks. Great.'

He gave me the address and said we'd be on the door.

When Billy got home from the warehouse, he was in a terminal state of mind.

'What if I don't feel like going out?' he yelled.

'You always feel like going out!' I yelled back.

Stomping about the house, he worked himself into an indignant fury.

'Why did he invite you, hey? Is there something going on? You fancy him, do you? I've heard he's hung like a horse.'

'He rang for you, actually, and he's inviting everyone, I think. It's nice. He's just being nice. And for what it's worth, I don't fancy him!'

Billy eventually calmed down, but I was beginning to notice a pattern with him. Some days he would lie in bed and refuse to get up or wash or eat. He talked about giving up, as though life were a hopeless waste of time. Other days he would have moments of whirling mania, wild bursts of energy that crescendoed into anger. I put it down to all the partying we were doing, but sometimes I wondered if there wasn't some underlying problem. On this occasion, after a drink and a back rub, he settled down and we caught a cab to the Cross.

The intimate little venue was out the back of a hotel I'd never noticed before. Watching Sex-on-Legs on stage was mesmerising and primal. He performed like a man possessed by the devil, raw sexuality pouring off the stage like hot magma. At the end of the set he leapt from the stage and came over to us, handing me a fake rose he had clutched between his lips.

Billy, being an astute sort of fellow, stuck close to me all night, but as I headed to the bathroom before making my way home, Sex-on-Legs bailed me up.

'Hey, I just wanted to say ... if you ever feel lonely or want some company ... call me. I'll come over for a cup of tea.' He handed me a slip of white paper with his number on it, stroked my palm and disappeared.

22.

For days, I rolled the piece of paper in my hands. I folded it. I smelled it. I memorised the telephone number and then finally, one Thursday afternoon, I threw it out. I was no shrinking violet, but I didn't have the guts or the cruelty to go through with it. Hurting Billy was the last thing I wanted to do.

But that night, with the crunched up scrap of paper still in the bottom of the waste-paper basket, I watched *Miami Vice* alone in the big old house, with all its creaks and groans. No house guests. No Joey or Jock. No Billy. Just me. Snuggled up on the cigarette-stained couch, cuddling a cushion.

Ten times I called the warehouse and there was no answer. I was worried about Billy. If he was going to be horrendously late, he always called. I fell asleep in front of the television until I was woken up by its static drone at two in the morning. Billy was still not home, so I dragged myself up the narrow staircase and curled up in bed, with the balcony doors wide open so that I could hear the squeal of the front gate. I missed Possum. She would have kept me company like a chubby mink stole about my feet.

I finally fell asleep to the insistent tinnitus of a mosquito.

At nine the next morning Billy phoned, sounding sick and sorry.

'Some of the guys dragged me out for drinks after work and we ended up back at Spider's and well ... you know Spider. I've only just dragged myself out of there and caught a cab back to the warehouse. They're shipping the bloody thing out at five and I've got a shitload of work still to do.'

'Hmmm,' I fumed into the phone. 'You could have called. I've been worried.'

'You're not my mother,' he grumbled and I wondered who the hell we were becoming.

'Fine. Fine.' I stood with the phone in my hand, wanting to hang up but also wanting the last word. 'Fine. You have a nice day.'

With a false sense of bravado, I decided to do the deed. But what if Sex-on-Legs really had meant a cup of tea? I paced up and down the hallway, having a monumental argument with myself that would have made Hamlet proud. Finally I reached for the old green phone and dialled.

The velvet voice answered. If his girlfriend had picked up I would have breathed a sigh of relief and hung up, freed from having to go through with it. I wanted this man so badly and yet I was afraid of the consequences.

'Hello?' he asked again.

'Hi …' I cleared my throat. 'Hi, it's me. Nikki.'

'Hey. Hi.' He sounded surprised to hear my voice. I was surprised to hear my voice.

'I was just wondering if you wanted to come over for that … cup of tea?'

The silence lasted only a few seconds but it felt like an endless tunnel.

'Ah … damn … I'm going to have to take a rain check, baby.' My mouth went dry, but it got worse. 'I'm working on the car today … it's an imported American beastie and we start recording in the studio tomorrow … Damn …'

I bit my lip and let the pride drain out of my body and down through the cracks in the wooden floor.

'Any other time,' he groaned.

'That's fine. I just ... well ... some other time. See ya.' I hung up fast, before I could hyperventilate.

I had never, ever been turned down for sex before and I felt a mixture of humiliation and dismay. Had I lost that invisible touch? I was no great beauty but I had a purr that seemed to register on most radars. But now? Nineteen and on the shelf! As I stared into space, trying to fathom it, the peal of the telephone invaded my trance and I jumped, grabbing for it.

'Stuff the car. I'm coming straight over.'

Argghhhh! Oh my God. It was going to happen. I couldn't go back now. Even if I panicked, I couldn't chicken out or I'd be that creature nobody loves, the most unforgivable of unforgivables – the Prick Teaser.

I quickly rang my friend Sam, who was working at a video store around the corner. My head was spinning and my nerves jingle-jangling.

'I might be going to do something that I shouldn't or might not want to do, despite at the moment wanting to do it, do you understand?' I blabbered.

'No, but why are you telling me this?'

'Because I need you to ring me at ten-thirty.' I looked at my watch. It was nearly ten. 'I need you to ring me and pretend there is an emergency and tell me that I have to go to your place immediately. Just ring me at that time and I'll do the rest. You know, in case I need an excuse to get out of it. The thing I might or might not want to do.'

A brief pause.

'Who is it? You have to tell me.'

'No-one. Well, someone. But no-one you need to know about. I'm just not sure I can do it, you know?' I trusted her implicitly and she knew that Billy and I were experiencing some tension. It was becoming apparent to those around us. Little snaps. Prods. Digs.

She stated her terms. 'I'll call you right on the dot, if you promise to give me all the details later.'

'If there's anything to tell,' I clarified.

'If ... yeah, right. Talk to you in half an hour.' She hung up.

I ran up the stairs, banging my shin painfully.

'Shit. Damn!' I cursed.

Into the bathroom. I'd already showered and dressed in anticipation of hanky-panky, but now I ran a face washer over my sweatier regions, reapplied my make-up and gave my hair an extra tease and spray.

Checking the bedroom, I closed the French doors, locked them and pulled the heavy drapes. No full daylight for me, thank you very much. Dim lighting for a first date – always. In only a few minutes I heard the low hum of a V8 engine and took a deep breath.

We sat on the couch and drank tea. Herbal, at his insistence. Knee to knee, beside one another, facing the television, which was blank and dead. The electricity was palpable. I had a chronic dose of stage fright and I guess he was waiting for me to make the first move.

'Do you have any hand cream?' he suddenly asked.

'Yeah, up in the bathroom ...' I began and stood up abruptly to get it. He stood at the same time and wrapped his arms around me. Standing there, arms dead by my side, I could feel the deep timbre of his heart, beating through his warm chest.

'I can hear your heart beating,' I said and then grimaced at my own cliché.

Slowly I let my hands creep up over his tight buttocks to form a knot at the base of his spine. Leaning back, I looked into his face and we kissed. He swung me into the air and I gave a hoot of surprise as he carried me upstairs, struggling a little under my weight. I directed him to the bedroom, where I landed on the bed with a bounce. We both laughed loudly as he flopped down beside me. After pausing a moment to collect ourselves he leapt back up, stripped all his clothes off and stood before me like a proud offering. I was more timid and let him undress me, shielding parts of my body with his own.

The sex was like a powerful current, dragging me under the surface of reason and sanity. Our passion crescendoed until at last fatigue won out and we collapsed into silence on the sweat-soaked sheets. I shut my eyes and listened to his deep breathing. My heartbeat was visible in my chest, my breasts moving to the cardiac metronome.

'Well, that was amazing,' he finally said in a hoarse whisper.

The phone beside the bed rang. Sam.

'Too late,' I mumbled and put it back down.

The phone rang again almost immediately.

'I'll talk to you later. I'm busy,' I snapped lazily.

'Hello, Nikki?' I didn't recognise the voice.

'Uh-huh,' I smiled, eyes roaming over the naked male body lying spent in my bed.

'It's Suzie Maizels, the casting agent. We met during casting for *Bliss*.'

All post-coital cosiness flew out the window. She had my full attention and I sat bolt upright, putting on my grown-up voice.

'Yes, Suzie, what can I do for you?'

'I'm casting a film at the moment. Based on a Peter Carey short story. I have a part that I think is perfect for you. Can you come in to meet the director tomorrow?'

'I'll be there,' I promised and hung up, elated.

A hand crept across the sheets like a pale tarantula and began tugging at my hip. I turned around and melted back into a passion I had no right or reason to be enjoying, a passion I knew would lead to pain, probably my own. But in those sultry moments, the need for pleasure far outweighed the fear of injury. I sank back into guilty caresses and felt the sharp edge of excitement slicing through my life. The madness of my libido had bolted from the stable once again.

23.

The director, Brian Trenchard-Smith, was a confident, amiable chap. His name meant nothing to me, but I was later told that he had an impressive reputation for making cutting-edge films. We chatted in Suzie's office for about half an hour, laughing and joking about various things until he gave me the nod and said, 'You'll do.'

Suzie smiled and showed me to the door.

'So when will I hear back?' I asked, unsure what the next move was and whether Brian's okay meant I would be granted a screen test.

'Oh, you've got the job,' she said. 'We'll courier you a filming schedule and the script. You start filming in about six weeks, don't you, Brian?'

'Something like that,' he nodded. 'We'll see you then.' He gave me a wink. 'Welcome aboard.'

I floated out to the waiting room, where Billy sat expectantly.

'I got the role,' I beamed. 'And I didn't even have to read from the script.'

'What do you mean?'

'I mean I got the role. I'm Shirl in *Dead End Drive-In*. It's a futuristic thing, like *Mad Max*.'

'Cool,' he said, and gave me a friendly slap on the back.

I was walking on sunshine for the next few weeks and let myself believe I could juggle my relationship with Billy and my affair with Sex-on-Legs. I threw myself into the fling like a crazed bungee jumper. Through a series of obsessive trysts, I alternated between deep, agonising guilt and the thrill of a wildly passionate secret life – two emotions I had long ago mastered.

'Hey, Nik, guess where we've been invited?' Billy blew into the house like a warm tornado one afternoon, calling out for me to get dressed. We were heading up to Surry Hills, he announced, to the recording studio where Sex-on-Legs's band was working.

'They want me to build something for their next film clip and asked me up there for dinner. They said it was fine to bring my missus along.'

I bristled at the term but gave an inward grin at the brazenness of my lover.

Rhinoceros Studios was tucked down a back street of Surry Hills, then a seedy inner suburb home to punks, deviates and homeless people, although even in the mid-eighties a small revival was going on. Townhouses were being bought and renovated by trendy yuppies with an eye to the future. The studio building, a concrete art deco office block, looked far more sombre and discreet than I imagined a rock and roll studio should. We climbed the stairs, knocked on the studio door and were ushered in. A handful of people lolled about and a couple of attractive girls were fussing in the kitchenette. I had never been inside a recording studio before and found it fascinating.

Looking down past the large glass coffee table, I immediately recognised Vivien, a small lady swallowed up by the large sofa. She was a mystical dark gypsy of a woman who had been a travelling companion of the Poet's band. She recognised me but was not sure where from.

'Where do I know you from?' she whispered into my shoulder as I took the seat beside her.

'Oh ... around the traps. You know.' I smiled nonchalantly.

'Hmmm,' she nodded wisely, her eyes glassy beneath the glossy black hair cut in the style of Cleopatra. 'Ahh ... I think I remember. You're a Persephone.' A knowing glint tickled the corner of her eye. A Persephone. So there were others. Perhaps I should track them all down and start my own band, the Persephones. I bristled, surprised that the memory of the Poet still held some power over me. 'He's somewhere in Europe,' she whispered, answering my unasked question.

Sex-on-Legs gave us a tour and got me to sit at the drum kit and hit it a few times.

'God, you're terrible,' he laughed.

Billy had a bash and proved to be more capable.

'If we ever need an understudy drummer, you're our man,' Sex-on-Legs smiled patronisingly. I squirmed, distinctly uncomfortable. My lover seemed to revel in the situation, letting a sneaky hand creep between my legs as he walked behind us, ushering us out of the studio and back into the lounge.

Dinner had been brought in and we tucked in hungrily, while Sex-on-Legs returned to the recording booth above. He stared down at us through the glass and I stole occasional glances at him.

Eventually Billy wandered off to talk to someone about his potential job. Seeing me alone, Vivien sidled up and asked me if I wanted a Rohy.

'What's that?' I asked naïvely.

'A Rohypnol. A pill. It's a really mellow ride.' She smiled sleepily. 'You'll like it.'

'A downer? I don't know,' I mused. 'You haven't got any coke, have you?'

'No, I took it all. That's why I need the Rohy. Usually I've got plenty, though. If you want some, I've got some arriving early next week. I'll give you my number. I'm down in Bondi. Right on the beach. Hey, you guys should come down and visit some time,' she raved in a gypsy trance.

'Sure,' I smiled. There was something sweetly maternal about her. To keep her company and to pass the time, I swallowed the tablet and it wasn't long before my legs began to feel like lead. The heaviness inched through my body until I felt I was melting into the couch. My mouth was dry and the room seemed darker. Thoughts came to my conscious brain five seconds after being generated. Even my vision seemed to have been set to some freaky time delay.

When Billy reappeared, I begged him to take me home. I could hear my bed singing to me like a faraway Siren. It was calling me home ... calling me to oblivion. Vivien said she'd share a cab with us, so we bid the rock boys adieu and I stumbled on Billy's arm out of the building, down past the old bus depot and up onto Oxford Street, where we managed to hail a taxi. It dropped Billy and me off first and spirited Viv into the night. I was asleep two seconds before my head hit the pillow, drifting into dreamless unconsciousness beneath my mosquito net.

The next noise I heard was an insistent knocking at my front door. The sound came from far away and then beat its way into my head, waking me like an early morning jackhammer. In a blur, I rolled off the bed, fighting my way through the mosquito netting like it was a giant spider's web and stumbling, fully dressed, to the balcony. The sun was high in the sky and there was no sign of Billy in the bedroom.

'Hello?' I called, my voice as husky as a bar-room blues singer.

'Hey there, Juliet,' called Sex-on-Legs, who stood in the front courtyard looking up at me. 'Little pig, little pig, let me come in, and I'll huff and I'll puff and you can blow ...' He laughed.

'Hang on,' I walked like an automaton, pulling my clothes off and stomping out of them, trying to untangle my feet without falling over. I grabbed a bathrobe and draped it about my nakedness, padded to the bathroom for a quick tooth-brush and shuffled to the front door. The keys were usually on the narrow hall table but the dish was empty.

'Hang on,' I called again and stumbled about the living room, frantically lifting magazines and records and ashtrays, looking for my set of keys. Suddenly I stopped. I remembered that Billy had left his at work the day before. He must have used mine to lock the front door ... from the outside. The front and back doors were both deadlocked. Without the key, I was a prisoner in my own house.

I went to the front window and pressed my face against the black iron bars.

'I think Billy's locked me inside. He's got the keys. I can't open the door.'

'Shit.' Hands on hips, he surveyed the balcony. It was a high climb, with only a few dead twigs to offer assistance.

'Have you got a ladder?' he asked. 'Out the back?'

'I don't know. The side gate's open. You can go and check. Come up over Joey's balcony out the back so no-one sees you.'

He could find no ladder. He made a half-arsed attempt to climb to the back balcony but couldn't pull it off. It was after lunchtime now and my stomach was growling, so I wolfed down a piece of dry white bread before meeting my lover at the back kitchen door.

We kissed through the bars of the ancient iron security grille. Running our hands over each other like lovers at the jail gates, our kissing became more inflamed and we tugged at each other's clothes.

'This might just work,' he laughed, unbuckling his snazzy cowboy belt buckle.

After some inventive and awkward oral play, we decided to do what we suspected no-one had ever done before in the hundred-year history of the house. In a slapstick routine, we managed to have sex through the prison door, with me on my knees, my lower legs jutting out through the bars, and him kneeling on the top concrete step. It was uncomfortable, hilarious and exhilarating.

'The bars have left bruises on my hips,' he laughed as I fell in a heap to the kitchen floor, panting with giggles. 'And your bum has red stripes like the arse of an exotic tiger. Red and white ...'

I made us tea and we sat, our heads pressed together through the iron divide as we chatted.

'I'm having so much fun. God, we're good together. But I do feel guilty. We're being very naughty.'

'But it's so goddamn good *because* it's illicit, don't you see?' he said intensely.

'I guess.' I retreated into thought as I watched a stream of orange leaves trickle to the ground from the tree behind him. He was so beautiful. I touched his cheek and felt terrible for what I was doing to Billy.

Common sense predicted that our union would not last forever. I knew what he was. A rock and roller with a massive libido – and I was not remotely interested in sharing a boyfriend. What we had was a fling, an exquisite erotic interlude that was bound to end soon enough. I could feel already that his attention had begun to wane. The world was his oyster and oysters were a powerful aphrodisiac.

I saw him only once more as a lover, when we laughed and beat ourselves against one another in a derelict building adjacent to the Pyrmont Bridge, thrilling to the sound of the distant cars. We saw each other occasionally after that at gigs and parties, but kept a polite distance. For a long and ruinous time I obsessed over Sex-on-Legs, grieving for that strange non-relationship we'd shared. Sometimes I would wake from a fitfully warm dream about him, suffering from tactile hallucinations.

I still loved Billy deeply and I berated myself constantly for having given in to such shallow urges. I'd wanted to have my cake and eat it too, which was exceptionally unfair. And like most secrets, this one was short-lived. Rumours spread quickly through the music scene and I stupidly, childishly, selfishly responded by admitting my sins to Billy. I thought it would be cathartic and enable us to wipe the slate clean. He coped with the pain without pushing me out the door and for a while our romance blossomed again. But over time my revelations became a thorn in our side that stung often, and hard.

24.

Filming for *Dead End Drive-In* commenced the same week as Sex-on-Legs left on tour. It was a well-timed distraction, and one I hoped would mark a new stage in my acting career.

Hoping to build on my first proper film role, Suzie Maizels had lined up an interview for me with the acting agency Bedford and Pearce, just over the Harbour Bridge.

'If you're serious about a career in film, you need an agent. I've put in a good word for you,' she enthused. 'You'll need to take a head sheet of photos.'

Billy arranged for a friend of a friend who was a professional photographer to do a photo shoot. I was nervous and self-conscious, but Billy lent me his leather jacket, complete with jagged patches where his older brother had come off a motorcycle, as a comforter. The few shots the photographer took of me in the jacket were by far the best.

With my new photos and a resume listing nothing more than a few high-school productions and eisteddfods, I turned up at their offices and was met by the gracious Shirley Pearce, an older woman with a head of grey hair and a youthful twinkle in her eyes. She had an inviting Pommy accent and I liked her straight away. The fact that I had already scored a small role in a feature film can't have hurt, and she agreed to put me on the books for a three-month trial. As I left, I perused the headshots of the shiny happy clients adorning the walls and was pleased to see more than a few familiar faces from TV and film. I felt another step closer to my date with Oscar.

My role as Shirl the Girl was not a large part, nor was it a very good part. I played a two-dimensional futuristic punk hairdresser who operated out of a public restroom. Nice! My character belonged to a small gaggle of girls and the other three actresses were a lot of fun. While I had few lines, we four girls were required to be in the background of many, many scenes. We were live scenery. There were no egos at all on set, not even from the leads, Net and Natalie, or from Wilbur Wilde, who probably had one of the bigger profiles of the cast thanks to his regular gig on *Hey, Hey, It's Saturday*.

We filmed on location in Matraville, a southern beachside suburb of Sydney. The set was a derelict drive-in that had been transformed by the crew into a punk wonderland. Hundreds of cars were decked out like makeshift little houses, adorned with clotheslines, deck chairs and antennas. A giant cinema screen hovered over the dusty lot like an ominous big brother. A colourful apocalyptic tableau, this crazy landscape was to be my home away from home for the next month.

On our first day on set, Brian sent us all to the wardrobe department, which was housed in the former cafeteria. A bubbly team of seamstresses and costume designers measured us up and gave us outfits to try on. Dressed in tracksuit pants and a loose jumper, I was horrified to be handed a tiny skirt made of woven seatbelts – only about four seatbelts wide. What horrified me most was that I was not wearing knickers. Too embarrassed to mention my predicament, I went into the change room and slipped into the clunky buckled number, which barely covered the lower curve of my bum. Topped with a hot-pink boob tube and a midriff leather jacket, I shuffled out to face the wardrobe mistress, my legs cemented together. She was ready and waiting for me with a Polaroid camera.

'Just turn around and let me get a back shot,' she smiled.

I turned to the left. Turned to the right. I could not bend over at all, not even an inch. After a lengthy examination and much discussion, I shimmied back into the change room and breathed a gushing whoosh of relief.

Safely back in my trackies, I met up with the others and we were ushered to the catering tent, where a generous lunch was waiting. I was on a film set, in a catering tent, hanging with professional actors as though I was one of them. I was a pre-fessional actress and it felt grand.

When it came time to film my scenes, everything I'd learned from Ray Lawrence went out the window. The stark reality of the set – lights, camera, action, and an audience of ten or twenty cast and crew just metres away – was unnerving for a novice. My awkwardness came across as shocking over-acting. Even worse, we had to go back into the studio a few months later to dub it thanks to poor sound quality on the original takes. Dubbing nearly always dilutes or distorts the original performance; while you can get the words to match the mouth, it can be hard to recapture the mood and significance of the moment. I guess it didn't matter ultimately, seeing my scene lacked any mood or significance to begin with! In true Ozploitation style, an assortment of stark-naked models soaped themselves up in the showers behind me while I fussed with another actress's hair at the sink. For any Australian film from this era with serious aspirations, some measure of gratuitous violence and/or nudity was essential.

As only a small percentage of the time on a film set involves actual filming, we had plenty of idle time on our hands. We filled it energetically, playing handball, pranking the older cast members and getting into the props for madcap productions of our own. Lusty unions took place between the cast and the extras, sometimes, rumour had it, in the little house-cars that dotted the set. It was a riotous atmosphere, enhanced by the explosions and other special effects. Security was constantly turning away petrol-headed hoons keen to crash the constant party.

Dead End Drive-In was a strange and complex work of art that I never really understood. The script seemed stilted, our performances were tripe and the whole thing was so kitsch it was impossible to take seriously. And yet the director did. Shakespeare this was not, and no Oscars would be won, but when it came to the action shots Brian Trenchard-Smith was a visionary. And in the finished product the clunky acting and stiff dialogue seem strangely appropriate. Crass and trashy, the film had a certain crazy charm, ensuring it a place on the 'cult classic' shelves.

By far the most memorable moment on set was the wrap party, which followed shooting of the final scene. The fire brigade was standing by and we were all required to gather for the bonfire of the century. A group of us had caught the bus out from the city, drinking a bottle of vodka on the way and well stocked with champagne to get us through the night. We'd been warned that the party could only begin after the final scenes were in the can and that this might take hours.

The shout of 'It's a wrap,' came not long before dawn. We had spent the last scene racing at a fire, pretending to put it out. We were screeching with laughter, which was supposed to be hysterical terror. Nearly everyone was drunk and we were all highly flammable; it's a wonder we didn't explode on set.

Once the fires had been doused and the burnt-out skeletons of cars lay steaming in the eerie first light, we straggled to the dressing rooms and took our garish outfits off for the last time. The whole place looked like it had been visited by the horsemen of the Apocalypse.

It was a surreal introduction to the world of movie-making. I had always loved the theatre, but film was fascinating and vibrant and if the cast and crew were right it was like being at a month-long party. It was with a heavy heart that I said goodbye to the Matraville drive-in.

On the domestic front, Billy, Joey and I were sad to farewell Jock from Boystown. He was headed home to the greyer but more lucrative pastures of the UK. We auditioned a host of potential new roomies before settling on a lighting man who went by the name of Virgil. In his late twenties, with a mop of brown curls that (despite his protestations) I always suspected was a perm, Virgil was new to the rock and roll life, having packed in a desk job to follow his dreams. He took to calling me 'Mum', a habit soon adopted by the other housemates. It was strange at first, but grew on me.

Billy and I were spending more and more time with Rhett, whose quick wit made me laugh more than anybody ever had. He was a clown, but there was a complex and sometimes insecure man behind the big brown eyes, a side he kept hidden most of the time. He was always good for a high, a low, or anything in between. We bumped into him one afternoon on our way home from Paddington Market.

'Come on back to Boystown with us,' I suggested, and he did.

After a few drinks, Rhett reached into his pocket.

'Hey look, guys, I've got a few tabs of acid. Forgot they were even there.'

Billy and I exchanged looks. I'd never tried it, but Billy had experimented years ago, before he met me. I'd heard about flashbacks and bad trips. People went mad on this stuff.

'Well, I'm not working tonight and we're not doing anything tomorrow,' Billy shrugged. 'I'm up for it if you are.'

'Yeah, what the hell. You only live once.' I said it like I didn't mean it, but I didn't want to be the one left behind while these two became silly.

'That's the spirit.' Rhett gave me a cartoon wink, located some scissors and began to cut up a sheet of paper that looked like a child's sticker set. He gave us each a tiny square with a picture of a little toadstool. It looked so innocent, like something out of my youngest sister's Holly Hobby books.

'Just put it under your tongue and leave it there for a while,' Billy said to me, popping one in his mouth. 'Then chew it up.'

I did as instructed and waited. I had another drink. After about ten minutes, I was getting a tad impatient.

'Nothing's happening.' I looked at the boys.

'Be patient, lovely,' Rhett leered, and I noticed that his eyes looked bigger. Definitely bigger.

Soon I was finding everything he said funny enough to induce tears.

'Where's your toilet?' he asked, and it sounded like he was speaking in a vacuum.

'Third star from the right,' Billy whispered.

'Upstairs and ...' I fell into a fit of giggles. Rhett disappeared and I decided to put the television on. The news was being read and I was struck by how much the presenter resembled a Freddo Frog. Billy wanted to play some music but kept dropping LPs out of their sleeves onto the floor, which was even more entertaining than the news. Rhett came back downstairs.

'Hello. Where did you come from?' I asked and we all fell about like lunatics in an asylum.

The memory of Joey coming home and yelling at us for the mess may be real or imagined.

'Shit. What's the time?' Rhett suddenly panicked. By this point time was very, very abstract.

'I've got to go up the road to see some friends. I promised,' he remembered, looking flustered.

So we all strode out of the house in single file, like the Beatles crossing Abbey Road. The sun was vicious and as we walked up Goodhope Street, my mouth was dry and I became disoriented. Clutching one arm each, Rhett and Billy almost dragged me up the slight incline. We ended up in a small side street where cars were parked on the footpath, wedged up close against one another.

'Look, it's a traffic jam and everybody's abandoned their cars,' somebody said into one or other of my ears. The footpath came to life as I stared, noticing things I'd never spotted before. There was a wilderness of activity down there. Ants. Lizards. Butterflies and bugs that had only just been discovered, by me. Sprouts of verdant grass leaped from the cracks in the baked concrete. The gutter must have been like the Gap to these creatures. Keep away from the precipice, I warned them. Stay close to the jungle and the fences. As we neared a house in Paddington Street, Rhett announced grandly: 'We are here.'

I sat on the footpath, still entranced by life in the gutter.

The door opened and Michael Hutchence stuck his head out, took one look at me and shook his head, smiling. Noise was spilling out into the street.

'Come on,' Billy called, 'there's a barbeque going on.' But I shook my head, rocking on the spot.

'Noooooo,' I hissed. Billy sat down beside me and Rhett shrugged and disappeared inside. I couldn't go in there. It wouldn't be right. There would be wall-to-wall musicians and I'd be contaminated by rock-star germs again. I'd put all that behind me.

Billy and I basked separately in the sun. He felt the need to protect me, which was comforting. We were cats. I was Possum. The spirit of Possum had entered my soul and I lazed on the pavement, licking my paws.

Finally Rhett reappeared, looking wild-eyed.

'Dull in there. What's happening here?'

I stretched languidly and I was no longer Possum; I was a cat-woman, like Natassia Kinski in *Cat People*. I was half woman, half cat, the same old me but with cat powers. I could leap and see in the dark and drink milk from a saucer. We wandered, arms interlocked, back down the hills and narrow streets towards home.

Suddenly I spied a kitten. It darted out through a gate and hid beneath a car parked on the road. It was a sign! Perhaps it was my kitten. Rhett laughed.

'Let's get Nikki a kitten,' he said slowly to Billy, who nodded ponderously back.

The three of us got down on our hands and knees and tried to entice the little fur-ball out to us. Here, kitty. Good kitty. Rhett fell to his belly and tried to slither under the vehicle like a hairy snake. The kitten looked afraid and made a run for home, but I pounced and caught it with my feline superpowers. It wriggled and scratched, leaving a jagged wound dripping blood from my hand. Aghast, I let it go. Once it had tasted human blood, it would only ever eat human meat.

Next comes a long blur in transmission, and then we are at Benny's at about nine o'clock that night. The clock in the corner is making a tick-tock noise for the first time ever. The place is empty. We sit in a booth and order water, because we're not sure if we have any money. Where are all the people?

'Maybe they're invisible,' suggests Rhett.

This makes perfect sense, so we begin to wave and say hello to them, so they won't know that we are tripping and can't see them.

Some time, possibly many years later, we emerge into the dark world outside to find a feathery drizzle wetting our faces.

'Fall-out!' cries Rhett and it all suddenly becomes clear. There really *were* no people in Benny's. There are no people left in the whole world. There has been a nuclear bomb and we are the only human beings left alive. We quickly get under cover. If we are the only people left on the planet, then Billy and I are the new Adam and Eve. What about Rhett? It reminds me of a silly riddle my mother used to tell me and I share it.

'Adam and Eve and Pinch-Me went down to the river to bathe. Adam and Eve were drowned. Who do you think was saved?'

'Pinch me!' Rhett yells triumphantly. I pinch him hard on the bum and he laughs hysterically.

The next day, I felt like I'd been trampled by a stampede.

25.

Christmas of 1985 was approaching. The city was bathed in candy canes and spray-on snow. Mum and Dad had sent us a Christmas card with money in it and I couldn't have asked for a better present. I toyed with the idea of paying up our growing cocaine debt to Vivien, but that didn't seem terribly joyful or triumphant. Deep down I wanted to use the money for a couple of train tickets to the Gold Coast. But Billy was working and we were helplessly dependent on one another; we couldn't bear the idea of being apart over Christmas.

This dependence didn't feel like passionate love anymore. It felt like claustrophobia. My infidelity had eaten away at Billy's self-esteem and he remained on high alert. I understood his insecurity. After all, I had inflicted it. But I felt like I was under constant surveillance. Worse, the paranoia worked both ways. I was in the red and he was in the black – he might have been plotting payback adultery. No way could I leave him behind for Christmas.

So, Sydney it was, and we decided we'd host a Boystown orphans' Christmas, a Christmas-eve do for anyone who found themselves away from home for the holidays. The Kiwis, Poms and Septic Tanks of Paddington were thrilled and as word spread, offers of help began to pour in. Pete, a licensed pyrotechnician who'd exploded things for the likes of Bon Jovi, David Bowie, INXS and Midnight Oil, offered to bring fireworks. Joey would set up the lights, turning our neglected backyard into a wonderland. Pinky and I put ourselves in charge of the menu and she combed through her cookbooks for the finest Christmas recipes.

'We could make rude food,' she suggested quite seriously, showing me a cookbook devoted to food resembling genitalia.

'Pinky, I'm trying to put on a classy party. No.'

'But some of these are classy. This one looks very nice.'

She passed me the book, which was open to a recipe for Toad in the Hole. I shook my head. But all in all, everything was coming together nicely.

When Christmas Eve arrived, we spent the day like worker bees preparing for a royal wedding. We were all up early for a change and even Pinky arrived before midday, decked out in a pink apron declaring her a 'Kitchen Slut'. It was her own design. While she began chopping and dicing, I cleaned the house from top to bottom. The bathroom needed some industrial-strength attention.

It was a perfect summer's day, not a cloud in sight. As the first blush of dusk crept into the sky, we surveyed the backyard with satisfaction. Red and green lights danced through the foliage and candles flickered on every table. We all dressed in our festive finest and assembled in the living room, awaiting our guests.

Rhett burst through the doorway first, singing a loud Christmas carol and bearing a bottle. Vivien was next, wearing a wreath of mistletoe around her dark head.

'Come and kiss me, boys,' she growled, and received several pecks on the cheek. As other guests arrived she grabbed me by the hand and led me upstairs. We went into my bedroom.

'Let's get this party started,' she grinned. 'Got a mirror?'

There was a gentle knock on the door and it opened a sliver. Just wide enough for Rhett to poke his moppish head into the room.

'Knocking on heaven's door …' he whispered.

'Come in, you big boofhead,' Vivien sighed.

She pulled out a small plastic bag and threw it into my lap. 'Merry Christmas, Persephone.' I let the name go because I was reeling at her generosity. There must have been three full grams there, about six-hundred dollars' worth. Rhett's eyes lit up brighter than the backyard.

'I'm moving to Melbourne next week. It's a farewell gift,' she said.

Rhett pulled an antique mirror off the wall. It had an ornate gilt frame around it, weathered but expensive-looking.

'Be careful, Rhett,' I cautioned. 'That belongs to the house.'

'Well, if I break it, I'll get the seven years' bad luck.'

I tipped a little powder onto the mirror and Vivien passed me a laminated video-shop card, which I used to break down the coke into six long lines. Rhett rolled up a twenty-dollar note and passed it to me.

'Merry Christmas,' I said and inhaled two lines, one after the other, one up each nostril. The burn. The taste. Lovely.

Pinky's food looked great and after a few joints had been passed around the yard, people were tucking in enthusiastically. The sound system was pumping and everyone seemed to be having a great time.

'Mistletoe!' shouted Rhett, swooping me into a surprise embrace and kissing me on the lips.

It was nice. I could taste the sting of cocaine in his mouth and wanted to let my hands run over his broad shoulders, but I stopped and pulled away.

'Tempting.' I licked my lips.

I caught Billy's icy stare from across the garden. Damn. Whenever he looked at me those days, I could see the suspicion in his eyes.

As the night wore on, guitars came out and a Christmas jam-band formed, made up of some of Australia's finest musicians. They christened themselves the Christmas Leftovers and rocked up a set of carols. At midnight we enjoyed the fruits of Pete's pyromania and a spectacular array of explosions burst over us, sending tendrils of smoke and the heady smell of gunpowder into the air. The grand finale lit up the sky and then whimpered back to earth, catching in the trees.

'Shit!' someone called. 'You've set the yard on fire.'

Flames leapt from the upper branches and someone raced to find a hose. Guests ran screaming as a powerful stream of water brought the night to a soggy end.

The next morning, I was first up to greet Christmas Day. I phoned home at first light, knowing the kids would be blistering to rip open Santa's gifts. After picking at unappetising leftovers for breakfast, I sat on the back step, dragging on a cigarette and blowing steam from my instant coffee. The heavy iron door was propped open from the night before; no-one had bothered locking up. There was nothing to steal but rubbish.

What would this new year bring, I wondered. Peace and trust in my relationship? My big break? Or just more partying? The sun burned into my shins and a neighbourhood cat fossicked through the backyard. Joey joined me and we began the clean-up, picking up discarded plates and glasses. No-one else stirred for hours and eventually I was all alone with my thoughts and a hangover. Silent day. Holy day. All was calm. All was bright.

Vivien left town. Rhett disappeared overseas for a stint. A few weeks into 1986 we watched, along with the rest of the world, as the Challenger Space Shuttle exploded. Glued to the television, I felt sick as the cameras panned across horror-struck faces. Kids all over the planet were watching. It was a horrible event and the media milked it for all it was worth, wringing every last drop of coverage out of it. In the end, we turned off the television and let the world grieve without us.

26.

After the high of my film debut, my acting career seemed to have stalled. Bedford and Pearce sent me for a few ridiculous cattle calls for television commercials, but I didn't present as the girl next door and that was usually what these ad monkeys were looking for.

Finally I was called in to audition for the part of a punk rocker. Now that was more up my alley. I pulled on some loud clothes, slinked a pair of fishnet stockings over my skinny white legs, frizzed my hair and slathered on the make up with a trowel. The result was suitably menacing and I landed the gig. The ad was part of a public-awareness campaign to educate people about the new threat of AIDS. My character was Vicki, a punk, who was sharing a couch with her equally spiky boyfriend, discussing the finer points of condom usage. The campaign was to be shown overseas and therefore paid top dollar. We celebrated with a bottle of cheap champagne and a big night out in the Cross. It happened to be my twentieth birthday, but I told no-one how old I was. Most of the Benny's crowd were five or six years older, and I did not want to be treated as the baby of the group.

With Vivien out of town, Billy and I needed a new dealer. For some months now I had shared a passing acquaintance with Jackie, an attractive blonde woman pushing thirty who was rumoured to be the unofficial coke-supplier at Benny's. This probably explained why Vivien had never joined us at that particular venue, preferring to haunt the corners of the Manzil Room.

It made sense now to get to know Jackie a little better, and we invited her over to our booth for a drink. She was clad as always in a white leather mini-jacket with fringed sleeves, matching white leather mini-skirt and white ankle boots. She was a cowgirl vision with perfect teeth and a glowing tan. Her sidekick, Brian, was a large, hairy man with a permanent scowl and close-set eyes. He didn't say much, but stalked behind his girlfriend like a personal bodyguard.

Ice-cold and remote as Siberia, Jackie was hard to read. Settled into our booth, she lit up a long, thin cigarette and threw her blonde mane over her shoulder.

'So, what's your story, then?' she asked, looking me up and down. I gave her the abridged version. When I told her I dreamed of living in New York, she leaned forward, blew a slow stream of smoke from the corner of her mouth and looked me in the eye.

'Me too. Want a line?'

'Sure,' I said. We made our way to the crowded restroom, squeezed into a cubicle and shut the door. The coke was smooth and clean and Jackie was generous. I must have said something right.

The rest of the evening unfolded as most of them did and we ended up at Baron's, with much sniffing and grinding of teeth and downing of doubles to help calm us down. Billy drew me into his arms, whispered 'Happy birthday, love', and I dozed in his lap as the party carried on around us.

The next day Billy filled me in on Jackie's story. Rumour had it that she was a former high-class callgirl who had been married briefly to a real underworld figure, a Sydney Al Capone. She had appeared in a spread for *Playboy* or *Penthouse* and Billy was keen to get his hands on a copy of that! We'd exchanged phone numbers and at seven that night, she rang and invited the two us to join her and Brian for dinner. For the next few months, we became inseparable.

'You guys are the first people who've made me really laugh in a long time,' she said to me one night. 'This scene can be depressing sometimes.' I realised that for all her partying, Jackie was a sad woman. She was intelligent, gorgeous and surrounded by friends – but she was lonely. She hid behind her body and her drugs. Were we alike, I wondered. Or would we be, if I stuck around the scene for much longer?

One night we were sitting around Boystown, waiting for the shriek of the midnight owl to tell us it was time to hit the Cross. Jackie left the room to make a telephone call and returned with bad news: there had been a big bust somewhere up the line and there would be no more coke that night. This put a damper on our plans somewhat.

'Come with me,' said Jackie, nodding my way. 'I know a guy who might be able to help us out.'

Leaving Billy and Brian behind, we crawled into her slick little white sports car and headed to Bondi Beach. We parked outside a nondescript cottage and I waited in the car while Jackie went inside. Fiddling with the radio, I found a good station and put my head back, closing my eyes as Simple Minds crooned, 'Don't you – forget about me.' When she finally reappeared, Jackie was looking worse for wear.

'He didn't have any. Only smack. So I got some of that.'

We drove back to Goodhope Street in silence. I had never tried heroin and the very word seemed poisonous as a scorpion.

It was the mother of all drugs, if you believed the legend. I wasn't keen, but I trusted Jackie and felt perhaps I should at least give it a try.

Back home, we snuck upstairs to the bedroom. Jackie went first, to show me that it was safe, which meant I'd be using her needle, although it had been fresh to begin with. She injected me and the rush almost knocked me down. I shut my eyes and swooned into a chair, then stumbled down the hallway to the bathroom. Heroin did not agree with me. I spent the rest of the night vomiting, retching until there was nothing left to expel but air and noise and the aching in my ribs.

The next day I woke to a burning brain and a creeping sense of self-loathing. I couldn't believe my own stupidity. I had crossed a line and I hated myself for it. Looking at my watch, I realised with horror that I was due in an hour at the AIDS shoot. I jumped into the mouldy shower, scrubbed at my regrets and slipped into my punk costume, then borrowed some money from the coin jar for a cab.

The shoot took less than an hour. 'It's not Shakespeare. Just bang out the lines and we can get the hell out of here,' was the director's approach. I liked his style. My flash-in-the-pan, blink-and-you'll-miss-it scene played out like this:

Two punks sit on a couch in a dingy living room, music playing in the background.

Boy has condom in hand and looks to girl.

'Hey, Vicki, I got a condom,' he says, sounding as thick as a plank of wood.

'Do you know how to use it?' Vicki asks.

'Yeah,' Thick-head replies.

'Well, now all you need is someone to use it with,' answers Vicki drily.

I was home by lunchtime. What a great spokesperson I was for an AIDS campaign, I thought bitterly as I crawled back into bed with Billy. Heroin was the last thing I needed in my life. I hated myself for sinking so low, and for having been so weak and gullible. Jackie was a dangerous friend, I realised. I wanted to reach great heights in life. I wanted my family to be proud of me. The mirror that morning had revealed a pale, spotty face and eyes streaked with red. Eyes like that could obscure the view. I needed to clean up my act and focus on where I wanted to be, instead of wallowing where I was. I needed to start looking at the stars again.

27.

Three weeks later, Billy and I were wedged into a booth at Benny's, discussing our dire financial straits. The problem with my work as an actress was that it took forever, sometimes months, before I saw a cheque. I was owed thousands for my couple of lines in the AIDS commercial, but who knew when we would see it. Work had been slow for Billy; many of his regular bands were overseas and INXS was on hiatus while Michael made his film debut in *Dogs in Space*. We were worried. But like a meteor barrelling out of the sky, fortune suddenly landed.

'Hey, guys,' smiled Mickey as she wiped up a wet patch on the table. 'I was going to ask you, Nikki ... we've got a busy period coming up with a lot of overseas acts coming to town, and we're going to need an extra pair of hands around here. Your name came up. We figure, you're here nearly every night anyway ...'

I cocked my head.

'You're offering me a job?'

'Well ... yeah. Just three nights a week.' She stood back with her hands on her hips, waiting for a response. I looked across at Billy, who had a lunatic grin splayed across his face.

'Say yes, Nik,' he urged me.

'We'll just have to discuss it for a bit, Mickey. I'll come down to the bar and talk in a second.'

'What the hell?' Billy exclaimed when she'd gone. 'Why didn't you just say "yes"? This is the answer to our problems. It doesn't get any better than this.'

'Because I don't want to work here.'

'Why not? The tips alone would be huge.'

'This is where I come to drink with our friends. I don't want to wait on them.' I felt awful about the idea. I knew it made sense to accept the offer and I'd probably have fun, but I didn't want to do it.

'You have to! We have no choice.' Billy was insistent.

'Okay. All right. I'll do it but I think it's a bad idea.'

Truth be told, I didn't want to be exposed to temptation every single night. How could I explain that to my boyfriend? I hadn't touched any illicit substances since hitting rock bottom with Jackie, and I hadn't looked lustfully upon another rock and roller since Sex-on-Legs. But I knew my weaknesses, and to expose myself to all my vices in my workplace would be a test I didn't want to sit. But Billy was right. Our financial woes demanded action.

I went downstairs and discussed the details and the deal was done. I would start the next night.

The first night was quiet and Mickey showed me the ropes. I'd never done bar work before so she had to teach me everything from scratch. Drinking was easier than mixing drinks, I discovered, taking it all in a little sullenly. I felt like a drink or a line. Sade's band stopped by after their show at the Entertainment Centre and ordered tequila all round. As I poured, I explained that it was my first night on the job.

'Then as part of your initiation, you must eat the tequila worm,' a cute guitarist demanded.

'No way.'

'Worm! Worm! Worm!' they all began to chant. I looked to

Mickey for help, but she'd joined in the chant. 'Worm! Worm! Worm!'

After some awkward digging around with a skewer, I managed to retrieve the bloated, dead creature and without a second's hesitation, put it in my mouth and chewed. It was cold and leathery and disgusting.

'Not the tastiest worm I've ever eaten,' I said with a saucy smile before sauntering back to the bar. The band cheered and hooted. I don't know if it was the worm's purported effects or the hundred dollars I'd made in tips, but I felt pretty good in the cab home at three-thirty.

Working from eleven at night until four in the morning was no great challenge, as my sleeping patterns had been on this crazy cycle for some time. Some nights Billy would accompany me to work and sit at the bar for the whole evening. He was just having fun, but I felt he was spying on me. Opportunities for mischief crossed my path nightly but I resisted.

So many celebrities were known by pseudonyms, it was amusing to take their American Express cards and see their real names, some of which were nerdy and embarrassing. Doc Neeson from the Angels accosted me on the stairs one night. He was a tall, imposing man and stood on the top step looking down at me on the bottom.

'My God, you're short. I always thought you were much taller.'

I laughed.

'No, really. You come across as this statuesque Amazon of a girl,' he charmed with the hint of an indeterminate accent, stepping down to join me on the bottom stair. He actually picked me up and stared into my face.

'You are a tall person trapped in a small person's body.' His eyes were aflame.

'Thank you, I think. And you're a Bernard, trapped inside a Doc's body.'

We both laughed and he planted me back down on the ground.

Michael Hutchence hung around a bit after he'd finished filming *Dogs in Space*. The rest of the band were scattered about the globe.

'So you're going to add movie star to your cap now, eh?' I asked.

'We'll see. It's a different gig and hard work ... but good stuff. How's your acting going?'

I was flattered that he'd remembered.

'I've got an AIDS commercial coming out on telly this week.'

Michael laughed. He'd been in a flat mood all night but this seemed to cheer him up.

'That is the most ironic thing I've heard for a while.'

'Thanks, buddy,' I laughed. 'Not as funny as if you were in it.'

During the day I continued to do the audition circuit. It was a world of knock-backs and humiliation. One day I was called in to audition for a Coke commercial. This was a golden goose. Coke paid top dollar and the ad would be shown all over the world. Unfortunately the brief required that I wear a swimming costume. That was not my style. My body hadn't seen the sun for years. I was alabaster white and sprinkled with orange freckles. I didn't even own a swimsuit. For two dollars I picked up a black one-piece at a thrift shop on Bronte Road and after shaving my legs and rubbing fake tan all over my body, I looked like a streaky cut of bacon.

The casting director, Liz Mulliner, had her offices in a cramped back alley behind Oxford Street. She was the queen of casting in Australia. I'd auditioned in front of her many times and found her to be a gracious and classy woman. She had been good to me and given me a lot of encouragement, but even she could not disguise her smile when I peeled off my clothes to reveal the marshmallowy, tangerine-smeared vision that was my body. I was lined up with a bevy of bleached-blonde Bondi babes and I wanted to crawl off and die of embarrassment. The looks of incredulity from the bimbo brigade were humiliating and I left with my self-esteem running down my cheeks. The tears didn't stop until I'd jumped off the bus in Paddington and run home to bed.

I'm not sure if she did it out of compassion or not, but Liz rang me the next day to tell me that while I wasn't exactly what the Coke people were after, she did have a job for me. She offered me forty dollars an hour to read opposite actors during a full day of screen-testing. So although I wasn't auditioning for the film *The Umbrella Woman*, which would star the dashing Sam Neill, I was being hired to read the role that would be filled by Rachel Ward. I jumped at the opportunity.

It was great fun to act without the pressure of auditioning. The director, Ken Cameron, was an encouraging guide and I learned a lot just listening to him mentor the stream of auditioning hopefuls. Over the next few months Liz called me in to do the same kind of work and the experience was invaluable. I got to meet such fine directors as John Duigan, John Edwards and Gillian Armstrong and I took something away from all of them. They were the key players in the Australian film scene and I longed to work with them on a real film one day. I did end up auditioning for a Gillian Armstrong movie, but the audition called for me to sing a verse of 'Viva Las Vegas' and it was not pretty. Sometimes being an actor felt like being a dancing monkey in a circus.

I did land one job on the ABC teen variety show *Beatbox*, playing Lindy Chamberlain – who had recently been found guilty of murdering her own baby – in a bad-taste skit. The make-up department transformed me into an exact replica of Lindy in a terrible brown pageboy wig, frumpy blue dress and dowdy make-up. I stumbled briefly into the wrong studio and gave the *Playschool* mob a fright. I was dubious about the verdict, believing the dingo truly had 'taken her baby', so I felt a little guilty about taking the mickey. I told myself it was a tribute.

Really I was a terrible waitress and spent more time gossiping with patrons than working. My shifts began to thin out and if it hadn't been for the spectacular tips, I might have thrown it in. I was determined to give up the job as soon as the elusive AIDS cheque arrived. Billy and I had been trying to embrace a more healthy lifestyle, although he was sometimes away on tour and I knew that his willpower was not made of steel. I was drinking less now; I figured all the booze I was pouring had turned me off the stuff.

One night in October, toward the end of a shift, I was shouted a drink by Grace Knight from the Eurogliders. We were standing at the bar discussing Scottish surnames with her friend, a film director, when I felt an overwhelming urge to be sick.

Within seconds I was leaning over the toilet, dry retching after flushing the vodka away. There were a few girls near the sink; they raised their eyebrows and gave me a wide berth. It occurred to me that I'd spent the last few days feeling vaguely off-colour. Maybe my liver had gone on strike. After washing my face and reapplying some bright lipstick, I wandered into the small kitchen out the back. It was run by a husband and wife team and I'd never had much to do with them before. I wasn't even sure if they spoke English.

'Hey, people. Could I please get a bowl of plain rice?'

'You want chicken? Pork?'

They leapt to their feet, overjoyed to be of service. I'd only ever seen them serve a handful of meals in all my time at Benny's. They were there chiefly to impress the licensing office, I supposed, as Benny's was officially classed as a restaurant.

'No, just plain rice,' I groaned, as another wave of nausea hit.

The two of them giggled behind their hands. I shook my head, missing the joke.

'You got baby, yes?' the man asked eagerly.

'What? No!' I pulled a face of disgust. Was I looking fat? I looked at my stomach. How rude these people were!

'My wife. She see things.' The weird little guy pointed to his eyes. 'She know things. You got a baby. Oh yes.'

He handed me a bowl of rice.

Back at the bar, I spooned it distractedly into my mouth. I was on the pill and almost always remembered to take it. When was my last period? Think. Think. With the crazy, drug-fuelled time I'd been having, I couldn't honestly remember. It seemed a distant memory. The rice filled the empty pit in my gut and I promised myself a trip to the doctor the next day for a test. Just to rule out the possibility. Another drama I could do without.

28.

The test came back positive.

'When was your last period?' asked the doctor, an elderly man who resembled Colonel Sanders from the Kentucky Fried Chicken ads.

'I can't remember. But I'm on the pill,' I protested. 'I can't be pregnant.'

He waved a dismissive hand.

'If you are sick or have diarrhoea or any number of things, it can affect your hormones. Interactions with other drugs ...' He gave me a judgemental once-over.

Not counting my current nausea, I hadn't been sick since the terrible heroin night. That was surely too long ago – but I had to admit to myself that my dedication to taking the pill had slipped into a whenever-I-remembered routine. After subjecting me to a thorough examination, external and internal, the physician disposed of his rubber gloves distastefully and sat behind his desk.

'I'll give you a referral to Dr Oscar H—,' he said, without looking up at me. 'I'm assuming you will be assessing your options. Do you know who the father is?'

I was offended.

'Yes, I'm in a relationship.'

'Well, Dr H— will help you with whatever you decide to do.'

I resented his casual disdain for what was a monumental moment in my life. His mind was already on his next patient, my situation having been scribbled away to become another doctor's problem. I was an unmarried young woman with too-big hair, too much make-up and a decadent wardrobe. Dr Dismissive wanted nothing more to do with me.

With great waves of trepidation, I told Billy the news over dinner at the Bondi Hotel. A grim-faced woman lobbed a plate of greasy fish and chips onto the laminex table and we smiled politely. Billy stayed silent, concentrating on his fish as he swam it about the plate in a sea of lemon juice. We managed a few mouthfuls and then strolled along the esplanade by the sand. It was a full moon and the sparkling crests on the waves looked like silver fish leaping from the dark water. I was reminded of home.

'What do you want to do?' he asked solemnly.

'What do you want to do?' I lobbed back.

We walked in silence for a few minutes while the sea breeze whipped our hair about our faces. A cold front blew up from the south and I shivered. My mouth kept filling with dry locks and I had trouble seeing where I was going. A punitive lashing. Billy passed me his jacket and wrapped a protective arm around me. Together we walked the entire length of the long curve of Bondi Beach, down to the baths and then all the way back north to the rock pools off Ramsgate Avenue.

'A baby doesn't belong in Boystown,' Billy considered carefully.

'We could move,' I said softly. I heard a seagull squawk and was startled because I thought they slept at night.

'But rock and roll and babies? I don't know. What about your Oscar?'

Tears pricked my eyes and I felt an emotional swell in my throat.

'Do you want me to just coat-hanger it? Is that what you want?' I stopped and my shoulders began to tremble as I tried to contain the torrent.

'No, honey,' he said, consoling me. 'I want whatever you want. I'm just warning you that I don't want us to get in over our heads.'

We stood, silhouetted against the grey sky and distended moon, holding each other forever.

On the fluorescent bus ride back to Oxford Street we held hands tightly, our thumbs massaging each other's fingers nervously.

'My parents will kill me.' I wanted to make them proud and this was not the way to do it.

'It's not about them.'

Billy was right, but I had not yet managed to shake the tug of my parents' disapproval. The umbilical cord stretched a long way.

'Let's think about it for a few days before we decide.'

That night I lay awake with my hands resting on my warm, flat belly. My thoughts returned to the night I had lain awake listening to fruit bats before the termination in Tweed Heads. I rolled away from Billy and let my tears fall to the pillow. Trembling beneath the weight of the decision, it was impossible to think clearly. Why did I feel so ashamed? I believed that women should have the right to choose. My life was important too. Billy's life was important. The little pulsing bundle of cells dividing in my uterus was a potential person, but until it had a heartbeat and a nervous system, did it count as a life?

A tree is a life. A leaf is a life. The fish and chips we'd just eaten were once alive. There are levels of life. An embryo is not a foetus or an infant. But I loved Billy, and the thought of the two of us creating a little version of ourselves was a magical one.

But I wanted fame and fortune. I had barely scratched the surface of my career. I wanted to be Madonna the rock star, not Madonna the sad-faced mother who had stared at me from church alcoves all my life. And yet the thought of having another embryo sucked from my body felt wrong. I certainly didn't believe in the God of my parents, the God of the Bible. I'd spent enough time in churches and confessionals, listening to men in purple robes and eating wafers, to know that no God in his or her right mind would be a party to that. But something like a whisper of morality stirred inside me. I couldn't always hear it over the noise of rock and roll, but lying inert in the cool spring breeze, the voice became clearer.

The voice was not a divine, booming echo from above but a small, gentle version of my own voice. It simply said, 'You know the answer. You are the answer.' And I realised with a bolt of revelation that God didn't make man in his own image; man made God in his image. Human beings had projected God out of ourselves like a laser-beam, producing a man with a white beard, a monkey with eight arms, a chorus of toga-wearing libertines, a warlike entity with no name, an earthy fecund woman and any number of other images. And when Jesus said the kingdom of heaven is within you, he meant exactly that. I was God. Billy was God. Mum and Dad and the kids were divine and even Rod Stewart was a deity (OK, I'd known that all along). I didn't need guilt or shame anymore because I realised that the only one judging my behaviour was me. If I was God I could bend the rules, break them or make them; my life was my creation and I made it up as I went along. I asked myself aloud, 'What do you want to do, Nikki?'

And I answered confidently, with tears swelling into sobs, 'I want to give this baby a life.'

The next day I walked the two kilometres up terrace-lined Liverpool Street, through Rushcutters Bay, past the bobbing yachts and up to the Edgecliff tower where the medical rooms were. Dr Oscar H— was slick, friendly and in his late forties. His smile was so inviting that I felt instantly relaxed with him. He was the antithesis of the cold and condescending doctor who had written me the referral.

'I want to have this baby,' I told him. He nodded thoughtfully.

'I'll examine you.' He pointed to a screen and asked me to undress behind it. After another thorough examination, he sat back down and slipped a pair of reading glasses onto his nose.

'Now, my dear, I would like you to have an ultrasound. That's where they put a device on your tummy and have a look at the baby. Your uterus seems larger than I would have suspected. I want to eliminate the possibility that you are carrying a multiple pregnancy.'

My eyes widened. There might be more than one baby growing inside me? I found the thought horrifying and amusing at the same time. As he wrote me a referral for the scan, I put the question I'd been dreading.

'I've had a few drinks ... a few too many. Will that ...?'

'My dear, do you realise how many women have taken this or that or got drunk or fallen down steps or any host of terrible things and gone on to have perfectly healthy babies?'

I shook my head.

'Nearly every one of them. So long as you take proper care of yourself from the moment you know you want to have this baby, you'll have not too much to worry about. Worry is the worst thing for you and the baby.'

The next day I fronted up to the ultrasound clinic on the second floor of a building on Market Street. I'd drunk a litre of water and held it in my bladder as instructed but I was ready to leak all over the waiting-room floor. My leg tapped impatiently and I silently begged someone to call my name before I had an embarrassing accident.

A few minutes later I was summoned and I bunny-hopped into the examination room. Up on the hard table, the radiographer exposed my marble-white belly and squirted a cool gel onto my skin. A television monitor stood in front of her and she turned it so that I could watch the procedure onscreen. A phallic device was rolled over my lower abdomen and immediately I could hear a noise that sounded like a rapid drumbeat.

'That's your baby's heart.' She smiled at me.

'So, I really am pregnant?' I asked, almost believing for the first time that this was not all a mistake.

'Not only are you pregnant, love, but your dates are a bit out. I'd be guessing you're about eighteen weeks pregnant ... nearly halfway there.'

I blinked back tears and breathed deeply. Fears came crashing down on me. The chemicals and abuse I had subjected myself to in that time were mind-boggling.

'Does it look all right ... I mean ... is it normal?'

'I'm just checking everything ... We can't give guarantees. But if everything is growing in proper proportion you're pretty safe to assume that all is well.'

She fiddled around and tapped on her keyboard. My mind churned thoughts and fears and dreams. I could hear the woman pointing out kidneys, bladders and lungs. I dragged myself back into the moment and looked at my baby's profile, saw its little hands open and close.

'You should be starting to feel movements soon,' she said.

'You're very petite, aren't you? Not even showing yet. But you'll pop out in the next few months.'

The reality of pregnancy began sinking in. I would swell to enormous proportions and then have to give birth. I looked at the little hands on the screen and wanted to hold them in my own.

I was twenty. I had no steady income and was questioning my relationship. I was obsessed with becoming famous. I had every reason to believe that a baby would be the worst thing for me right now and yet I felt utterly compelled to embrace it.

I rang Billy at work as soon as I got home. I had a black and white ultrasound picture of our child. It looked like a grainy grey wave with the curve of a profile and a small foot.

'How many heads does it have?' he asked.

'One head and two legs and two arms and it's perfectly healthy and I'm nearly five months pregnant.'

Silence.

'Billy?'

'Shit,' he mumbled. 'Well, what are we going to do? Your call.'

'We're going to be a mummy and a daddy,' I cried into the phone.

'Super.' He sounded almost pleased.

Billy brought a teddy bear home and we laughed and cried at the same time.

I went back to Dr Oscar.

'Your due date is February 8th.'

He stood up, came around his desk and wrapped his arms around me.

'You will make a wonderful mother. I can tell these things,' he whispered, and I thought in that moment that I might call my child Oscar if it were a boy. There would be the added bonus of being able to say quite truthfully that I had an Oscar! He wrote me a script for an iron supplement and told me to rest up and eat well.

At home, I lay on the couch and ran my fingers over my not-quite-flat belly. The doctor had shown me the hard ball that was just beginning to peek up and out from my pubic bone. My breasts had become larger and harder. I was surprised that neither Billy nor I had noticed. Shutting my eyes, I traced my growing womb. At that moment I felt a tiny ripple, bouncing like popcorn beneath my fingers. Another bump with a little more force, and then stillness. I sat up, breathing deeply. This was real. I was not dreaming. There was a living person growing inside me. Not a blob of cells, or a bacterial infection. A person.

After much rehearsal, I rang Dad from the bedroom and calmly told him the news. His reaction was anything but calm and he tried to persuade me to think of alternatives, a funny line for a Catholic to take, I thought. I begged him to break it to Mum gently. I didn't want her to panic.

'Dad, I've finally got my cheque for the AIDS commercial and we've found a nice unit in Bellevue Hill. The money will help to get everything ready. I've got a great doctor and we are really, really happy, so please just accept this.'

He had to accept it, of course. Mum surprised me by ringing the next day and giving us her stilted and frightened blessing. I knew what was going through her head but she had the grace not to share all of her concerns with me. She pretended to be excited and almost convinced me that she was.

'Why don't you come home, Nikki?' Her voice cracked and I had to say goodbye before I broke down. I couldn't go home. Not yet.

29.

Two days later I heard that I'd been cast in a Yoplait commercial. I was to play a Moulin Rouge dancer in a sequinned blue leotard with a massive feather headdress. That made Billy and me laugh.

'Good thing you're hardly showing. They might not like a pregnant can-can girl, hey?'

The commercial was filmed in a big warehouse and I felt like a croquembouche, strutting around in my sequins with a monstrous great peacock on my head. There was a man in a gorilla suit who had it worse than I did; he had to arrive on-screen by flying fox. The Yoplait man was famous for his line, 'Yoplait ... it's French for yoghurt.' I had seen him on TV countless times and was surprised to find he was a real Frenchman who had been flown to Australia especially for the shoot. In one take the gorilla collided with him and sent him flying. He was briefly unconscious but soldiered on through the afternoon, saying 'Ze show must go on' in his thick French accent.

My scene saw me in a jail cell, bending the bars to accept a tub of yoghurt. I spooned a dollop into my mouth seductively as the French gendarme said, 'Stay as sweet as you are, Simone.' Just one problem: I hated yoghurt. Particularly warm yoghurt. Particularly as I felt nauseous with hormones. Between takes a crew member passed me a bucket into which to spit the crap. But the commercial paid well, which was lucky: I would surely be showing soon and there weren't too many roles for pregnant women about.

My stomach started popping over my belt not long after the Yoplait shoot. Shirley from Bedford and Pearce was congratulatory, but warned me not to tell any of the casting directors. At my age, this could put the brakes on my career with a rubbery squeal. I promised myself that I'd get back into shape fast once the baby arrived. Pregnancy would be only a brief pause in my journey toward Oscar.

Billy and I packed up our belongings and said goodbye to Boystown. Joey had recently fallen in love with an American girl and was leaving the country. Virgil had also fallen in love. So with a small celebration and little fanfare, Boystown closed its door to rock and roll and retired, becoming just another stately terrace house in Goodhope Street, Paddington.

We were moving to a two-bedroom flat, clean and renovated, on the top floor of a large brick block in Victoria Road, Bellevue Hill. My fee for the AIDS commercial paid for a collection of second-hand furniture and while Billy toured with Icehouse, I spent my days pottering around the neighbourhood thrift shops in search of little treasures. It became my new addiction; I could hardly go a day without a fix of Lifeline or St Vincent de Paul.

Jackie and Brian and our myriad of other acquaintances would drop in for tea or coffee now and again, but without the high of cocaine we had little in common. One afternoon Jackie invited us over for lunch. As I applied my lipstick and climbed into yet another outfit that resembled pyjamas, I sulked.

'I don't feel like going out. You guys will drink and they'll probably offer you some coke.'

'Don't be like that. They're our friends. I'll take you to the movies after lunch, how about that?'

By three o'clock he was wired off his dial and he and Brian were onto their second six pack of beer. Jackie was making no sense and was showing me her famed centrefold spread, which only made me feel like a deformed whale.

'Movies,' I whispered to Billy, elbowing him in the side.

'Boring.' He made a face at me.

I pushed myself up from the couch and stormed out, slamming the door behind me. Walking down William Street from Kings Cross, I got two wolf whistles and three horn honks. Some people were perverse! Checking my handbag, I found that I had enough cash to go to a movie myself. I had never ever gone to the cinema alone.

The cinema on Pitt Street offered little that appealed to me. I opted for *Malcolm*, a small Australian film. One of the actors was a regular at Benny's and I'd shared a couple of drinks with him. The flick made me completely forget my anger at Billy and I laughed out loud. The baby kicked in my belly and I realised that I was not alone after all. I'd just taken my son or daughter to the movies.

Out in the foyer after the film, I stopped in front of a poster advertising the opening the following week of *Dead End Drive-In*. My small headshot appeared in the lower left-hand corner. Billy might have missed *Malcolm*, but he wouldn't be getting out of a trip to the movies the following week.

After the final credits rolled and my name had flashed quickly by, we walked down George Street, looking for somewhere to have dinner. Ten minutes passed wordlessly until Billy finally spoke.

'I'm sorry, Nik, but that was truly awful.'

I laughed, but inside I was devastated. My film debut might just go down in history as the worst performance of all time. I saw my Oscar evaporating before my tear-blind eyes. I'd looked awful. I was playing a terrible stereotype – the gum-chewing slut – and I didn't even do that well. My dialogue was wooden and my facial expressions suggested constipation. The final scene was impressive but the rest of the movie was all tits, punks and car crashes. I wondered why I should bother ever acting again.

As my belly grew, Billy began going out on the town more and more without me. I had no desire to go clubbing or gigging. More often than not he didn't come home until the first light of morning. One night I sat for hours in the laundry basket in a corner of the darkened bedroom, listening to Crowded House on my walkman. In the morning Billy straggled in, looking like the wild man of Borneo.

'I walked home through Cooper Park, but I was trashed and must have passed out. I woke up under a tree because some kid was kicking me, yelling, "Mister, are you alive?"' Billy thought it was hilarious. I was worried and hurt.

I read every book on pregnancy I could get my hands on. I learned about Braxton Hicks contractions and stretch marks and haemorrhoids. It was a messy-sounding business, but fascinating. Being short with a small build meant that very soon I was a walking belly. The baby wriggled and kicked all night, keeping me awake. I talked to him or her and collected singlets and stretchy jumpsuits in neutral yellow or white. I rolled through summer like a hot, throbbing bunion.

We had a huge window in our bedroom, overlooking busy Victoria Road and Cooper Park beyond. Billy would catch the early morning bus to the city and then another to Pyrmont, where he was working in a factory, making props for film and television and rock clips. Every weekday morning I would sit on the bed and wave out the window to him, using sign language to express our love or whatever else was racing through our minds.

One morning, much to his consternation and the amusement of others at the bus stop, I stood up in just my knickers and pressed my eight-month belly and gigantic mammary glands against the glass.

'That was funny,' Billy said through a mouthful of pizza that night. 'Just don't do it again.'

I began attending antenatal classes at St Margaret's Hospital in Darlinghurst. Most of the women were accompanied by their partners but Billy was often away and if he was at home, he slept for much of the day.

'It's not really my cup of tea,' he said when I asked him to come along.

At the first class I was dubious. I was prepared to give it a go but didn't see why I couldn't learn whatever I needed to know from a book. People had been having babies forever. It was a natural process, like sex – and we hadn't needed lessons for that.

We sat on the floor in a circle, four couples and one other single woman and me. She and I were paired up as a makeshift duo. She was a beautiful blonde Englishwoman with the creamy complexion that comes from living in a climate of drizzle. Ever a sucker for an accent, I got goosebumps when she spoke. We introduced ourselves and exchanged quick resumes. She was nearly thirty and had lived in London, New York and Athens. This was fascinating in itself, but then I learned she was an artist. A painter. Her work hung in galleries around the world. I shared the meagre details of my acting career.

'I'll have to see *Dead End Drive-In*,' she smiled, revealing gorgeous teeth with a wide gap between the top two. I had always hated the gaps in my teeth but on the Artist, it was striking. Her smile shone like a proud frame around it.

'Please don't,' I laughed. 'I think it shut down after the first week, anyway.'

After we'd practised panting and breathing and watched a horribly graphic film, the Artist invited me for coffee at the hospital cafeteria.

'I let myself have one coffee a day,' she told me as we waddled together through the sterile corridors.

'Where's your husband or partner or whatever?' I asked.

'I'm doing this on my own,' she said. 'I asked a friend for his sperm and he gave it to me, no strings attached.'

'Oh, right …' I nodded. 'Will your friend be a part of the whole parenting thing?'

We sat down and ordered coffees.

'No. He doesn't want to be involved and that's fine. If he changes his mind, I'll be happy to share the experience with him, but he's gay and heavily into the New York art scene.'

We enjoyed each other's company and decided to commit to the six-week course as partners and coffee pals.

That same afternoon, Shirley Pearce called me.

'Ken Cameron wants to meet with you to discuss a role in a telemovie. What should I tell him?'

Ken was the director of *The Umbrella Woman*, which I'd worked on as a stand-in reader during auditions. I remembered him as a lovely, genuine man and felt sure that he could handle the truth. Perhaps filming was more than four weeks away.

'Just tell him the truth and see what he has to say.'

I met with Ken the following week. On my way in, I passed a girl on the stairs with rich, brown hair and pretty eyes. She looked familiar. And then she smiled at me with a mouthful of lovely teeth.

'Gia Carides,' I said out loud, and felt instantly embarrassed.

'Have we met?' She smiled again.

'No,' I mumbled.

'Good luck with the baby,' she said, nodding to my stomach.

'You have lovely teeth.' I couldn't help it. It escaped from my lips like a sneaky burp.

'Thank you!'

'And I thought you were great in *Bliss*.'

She was lovely. As I continued up the stairs, I couldn't help but jealously mouth the word 'bitch'.

'That's some belly,' Ken laughed as I was shown into the room. 'And the million-dollar question is, when are you due?'

'Three weeks.'

'Perfect,' he clapped his hands together. 'We start shooting in five. Here's a script. It's a piece on police corruption called *The Clean Machine*.'

'Do you want me to read for you?' I asked.

'Not necessary. It's only a small role and I'm sure you'll be perfect for it.'

I was over the moon.

'You'll be working closely with Grigor Taylor,' he continued.

I stared at him. I had suffered from a massive crush on Grigor when he'd starred in the television series *Glenview High*.

'That's great. Grigor is great.'

And then Ken added, nonchalantly: 'Oh, and are you okay with nude scenes?'

Time froze like a pause button had been hit.

30.

All my thoughts were now focused on our due date of 8 February. For days on end I played with Tarot cards, trying to determine when my baby would be born. The tail end of summer was ruthless and I lolled on the couch, bathed in sweat.

On 25 January, Billy and I attended a secret gig by INXS at the Tivoli. 'This will be my last night out for a while,' I warned him. It was nice to put on make-up and dress up for a change, and I swathed my grossly swollen frame in a full-length red jacket. As we lined up to get in, a couple of young guys sauntered up behind me, singing the Stevie Wonder hit 'The Woman in Red'. When I turned and flashed my rotund gut at them, they reeled back in surprise.

The Artist and I continued to enjoy our classes together and after our fourth lesson, she asked me back to her flat in Bondi for tea. We struggled into her little MGB and drove down to the ocean. She lived in a ground-floor unit, rich with colour and character. The walls were painted white and the floor was covered in mosaic tiles, blues and purples and silvers. It was a shimmering wonderland. Her paintings lined the walls and her sculptures adorned the mantelpiece. I followed her into the kitchen.

'Iced tea?' she asked. 'We'll sit in the garden.'

Outside, her courtyard was overflowing with plants and

herbs and impossibly vibrant flowers. We sat on a hand-woven South American rug.

'Here, I'd like you to read this. It really changed my life.' She handed me a book. *My Mother / My Self*, by Nancy Friday. 'I think it will change your life too. It's a gift. For a new mother.'

She leaned across the rug and kissed me on the lips. As gentle as a cat's whisker, the kiss lingered two seconds longer than a friendly peck should last. She looked into my eyes and I could see my wide-eyed reflection in them. A milky little me swimming in her sea-blue irises.

'Thank you,' I smiled. Not embarrassed. Not guilty. Just flattered and grateful.

She lifted her white cheesecloth shirt and lay back, letting the sunlight bathe her extended belly. The silvery stretch marks ran in concentric patterns around her lower abdomen like a large rosette. I reached out instinctively and touched it. Warm and hard. I felt her baby stir beneath my hand.

'So beautiful,' I murmured and lay down beside her.

We lay there watching the clouds swirl and dance across the pale blue sky. A gust of wind sent a sprinkle of leaves over our bellies and we laughed. A few seconds later a sudden sunshower began to fall. We ran inside like lumbering white elephants and settled in the living room.

'Music,' she laughed. 'We should dance. The dance of the fertility goddesses.'

I hadn't danced in ages. At gigs the most I ever did was bounce about rhythmically. A flutter of acoustic guitar filled the room and I imagined a dark, pony-tailed Spanish man fingering the fret board. I shut my eyes and let the music move through me. The child in my womb began to sway. My arms snaked through the air and my feet moved as if on water. Together we swirled and I felt the power of being pregnant.

'I'd like to paint you,' she said after the music had stopped. 'I'd do a self portrait but I can't find a mirror big enough.'

I nodded. Usually I was uncomfortable with my nakedness, but with a nude scene coming up I figured I could use a dress rehearsal. Or lack-of-dress rehearsal. In the telemovie, I would be sitting naked on a bed. Ken had promised to film the scene from behind to make it easier for me.

The Artist had me recline on her blue velvet couch and I felt quite Rubenesque. I was a little embarrassed by my appendectomy scar, which had grown into a purple welt, but I shut my eyes and let myself relax.

'You're beautiful,' she said as she went to work at her easel. It had been a long time since Billy had told me I was beautiful. As I lay there, we talked of many things. She told me about the streets of New York, painted me a mental picture of a city that felt like home to me. She told me about her lovers in Greece, her parents in Coventry and her brush with breast cancer. I told her about my teenage deviance, my love of theatre and my dreams of fame and fortune.

'Do you think I'm shallow for wanting to win an Oscar?' I asked.

'No. Everyone should have one grand passion.' I opened my eyes and smiled. So long ago I had seen the same words on a bumper sticker and adopted them as my motto. Back then I had thought my grand passion was rock stars, but now I saw that they were just entertainment on my journey to a grander goal.

'I will win an Oscar one day,' I announced, more sure than I'd ever been.

'Of that I have no doubt.' She smiled. 'But our passions don't always come to us in the form we expect. Remember that.'

The afternoon turned to dusk and I stood at her door.

'You can see the painting after I've finished. I just have some shading to do. I'll hang it in New York for you one day. Some quirky little gallery.'

I smiled and leaned forward, kissing her deeply on the lips. We let our hands rest on each other's bellies. This wasn't sexual but sensual. I discovered that something physical could pass between two people that transcended sex.

'See you in class,' I winked, and caught a cab back to Bellevue Hill.

That night I began reading *My Mother / My Self* while Billy was out constructing a stage for a gig at the Entertainment Centre. It was eye-opening stuff and I wondered how the Artist could possibly have known how apt Friday's book would be to my life.

My Mother / My Self was subtitled 'the daughter's search for identity', and it hit me like a slap across the face. This was what I had spent my youth doing – searching for my own identity, sorting through the various labels on offer: daughter, sister, schoolgirl, friend, lover. I had been born into a revolutionary world for women. The free-loving hippies had paved the way and the pill had liberated us (not that I was very good at remembering to take it). But growing up in a conservative Catholic household, I had no female sexual models to look up to besides Mary Magdalene. All I had were celebrities – movie stars and rock and rollers – to teach me about passion and sensuality. The only books about sex I had read were old anatomy texts like

Everywoman. Nancy Friday's book showed me the missing link: she delved into the emotion and psychology of sex, pointing out that my generation was facing a new world and navigating a new sexual landscape. Instead of feeling like a freaky little slut, I realised, I could consider myself a revolutionary. A pioneer. I started actually liking myself.

I had been brought up to think of my sexuality as something shameful. It was a curse shared by many if not most of my gender. The Catholic Church had long decried the female sex and this message had been hammered home in every religion lesson I'd attended. When my hormones had struggled to life in my teens, I'd been wracked with shame, guilt and confusion. I'd thought I was a freak of nature, a disgrace. Perhaps I had targeted 'idols' – iconic symbols of sexuality – thinking that if they could want and love me, then maybe I was a desirable, loveable creature. They validated me. Then again, perhaps I had sought out rock stars because they were considered sexual deviants; maybe I was seeking out my own kind.

I lay awake all night, tossing in a psychoanalytical haze. I swam back into my childhood, remembering the little girl who'd been so confused and had felt so alone in her confusion. I touched my belly and promised my baby that I would never judge, never condemn. I would always be there to listen to fears and I would never, ever reject or stifle the person he or she wanted to become.

31.

By the thirteenth of February I was irritable and impatient. The Artist had not been in class that day and I'd gone to the maternity ward in case she'd had her baby. She was due a few weeks after I was. But she wasn't there, and I realised with dismay that I didn't even have her phone number. I arrived home to an answering machine message from Dr Oscar; he'd induce me the following Tuesday, he said, if nothing happened in the interim.

And then I received a phone call from the wardrobe department of *The Clean Machine*.

'Hi, Nikki, this is the wardrobe mistress … just quickly, can I get your measurements? Chest, waist and hips.'

I don't know if she heard me laugh. What should I say – 200/700/150? I decided to project a nice set of optimistic post-pregnancy statistics and went with 36/25/34. I couldn't have known how naïvely hopeful that was.

Billy came home from work with flowers to cheer me up.

'Hey, gorgeous,' he smiled as he boiled the kettle for yet another cup of rosehip tea, 'The Angels are playing tonight for black Friday. The gig's called Howling at the Hordern. You know, Friday the thirteenth and all that. I've got passes. You could say hi to Bob.' I could tell he was itching to go. I had nothing better to do and figured a good blast of rock and roll might be just what the baby needed to get things moving.

'Sure,' I nodded. 'Let's go.'

I'm sure I was the most pregnant woman ever to stand

stage-side, next to an enormous amp. Doc Neeson dedicated 'We've Got to Get Out of This Place' to my unborn baby – but despite the mega-decibels, he or she stayed firmly in utero. The band played well but Doc seemed tired and Bob appeared tense. I was starting to look at rock gigs with a jaded eye. It was really just a bunch of blokes, gyrating and making a lot of noise. I wanted to get home to bed to finish my book.

Nothing did happen in the interim, and on Tuesday morning we woke at 6 a.m. I nervously packed my toiletries into the top of my overnight bag, which had been sitting ready by the front door for over a month.

'Happy birthday, my darling.' Billy kissed my ear. It was my twenty-first birthday. Fate had a sense of humour. Maybe today would see me finally grow up.

St Margaret's was a private hospital. I was admitted as a public patient but with my own private doctor attending. We'd saved relentlessly for the room, which cost a whopping three hundred dollars a night. I might as well have given birth in the presidential suite at the Hilton. Up on the third floor, we were ushered into a delivery suite. While I waited for a nurse to come, I wandered around, looking at the alien furnishings. There was a small plastic crib on a trolley with a blanket folded neatly at the base. I touched it and thrilled at the idea that my son or daughter would soon be snuggled under it. There were oxygen tanks and masks and a machine with all sorts of leads and buttons and lights next to the bed. A drip was set up on a stand at the head of the crisply linened metallic bed. Billy had gone off to the cafeteria to find some breakfast, leaving me to endure the humiliation of an enema and a shave.

We'd spent months discussing possible names for our child. I liked Brittany for a girl. I'd heard that Lyn Baron, the super groupie from that first Australian Crawl gig, had gone on to marry Christopher Atkins from *The Blue Lagoon*, and that they'd called their first daughter Brittany. It was a province of France and I thought it a beautiful word. Elizabeth was another more old-fashioned contender. I was a little obsessed with Elizabeth I, Tudor queen of England. Boys' names had been harder to settle upon. I liked Oscar but Billy hated it. The one name we did agree on was Benjamin. I loved Biblical names, and this one wasn't as common as Matthew or Joshua, which were topping all the name charts in 1987. Michael Jackson's 'Ben' – written for a giant rat in the horror movie of the same name – made me cry the first time I heard it. And of course, there was Benny's.

Billy returned to the delivery room with a *Countdown* magazine for me and a Snickers bar for himself, just as the nurse slipped a cannula into my wrist and attached the drip, which began to drizzle synthetic oxytocin into my bloodstream. Doctor Oscar appeared with his flashing smile and wished me a happy birthday.

'I'll give you your present later today. A beautiful baby.' He winked and went to attend to a patient in the next room. She was already making noises that sounded unpleasantly like pain.

Within a handful of minutes I felt a strong tightening in my abdomen and a sensation like someone had drawn a wire about my belly and pulled. It wasn't exactly painful, just uncomfortable. Another nurse appeared with something that looked like a crochet hook.

'Okay, sweetie. I'm going to break your waters so that Bub can get a bit more motivated to come out. This usually speeds things up a bit.'

She got me to flop my knees apart and poked around inside me until she found the cervix. Then she gave the baby-bag a nick. It was not pleasant at all and with frightening suddenness, a veritable bucket of fluid rushed from between my legs. The uncomfortable tightening sensations grew in intensity and began to sting.

'Just breathe,' Billy reminded me, as if I were likely to forget. He held my hand and watched the machine beside the bed. I had a belt wrapped around my giant girth, monitoring the length and magnitude of my contractions.

'Whoa,' Billy sounded impressed. 'That got up to sixty-three.'

Three hours passed, punctuated by increasingly acute pain, but I prided myself on my stoic resilience. The machine was registering over one hundred. The woman in the next room was groaning and grunting and sounded like a bad porno actress doing a very over-the-top rendition of an orgasm.

'If I end up sounding like that, gag me,' I laughed, before grimacing at another pain.

Dr Oscar strode into the room, all smiles, and checked my dilation.

'Only two centimetres,' he frowned. 'You're going to get too tired. This might take a while. I suggest you have an epidural.'

I was dubious. Mum had warned me that she'd read about women being permanently paralysed from the waist down. But Dr Oscar dismissed my fears.

'I wouldn't suggest it if I wasn't one hundred per cent sure you needed it. It's completely safe.'

I trusted him implicitly and agreed.

'It might relax you enough to get some dilation happening.' He smiled and nodded to the nurse to call the anaesthetist. At that moment, after a guttural howl from next door, the feeble cry of a baby crept into the room.

Sitting perfectly still on the edge of the bed, I bit my lip as the anaesthetist gave me a local anaesthetic before inserting the spinal block.

'Holy mother of God, look at the size of that thing,' Billy whistled. 'Nik, it looks like a bloody horse needle.'

'Thanks for that,' I mumbled into my chest, curling into a prayer that all would be well.

Within a minute I could no longer feel my toes or my legs. Billy kept pinching me, thinking it was funny. I tried to read *Countdown* but found it hard to concentrate. The contractions were still coming fast and furiously according to the machine beside the bed, although I felt nothing but a dull tightening. Eventually I fell asleep.

Two hours later, I woke with an odd sensation between my legs. A pressure was exerting itself against my colon and I thought perhaps I needed to go to the toilet. My face felt hot and a little voice in the back of my head whispered that my baby was trying to evacuate. A nurse doing the rounds came in for a routine check of my progress.

'I'm fine. Nothing happening here,' I hurried to inform her, suddenly terrified that the birth was imminent. She did a quick inspection of my nether-regions and grinned up at me.

'You're ready to push. I can see baby's head.' She called on the intercom for Doctor Oscar and everyone seemed suddenly animated.

Billy's face was flushed and he put aside the tuna sandwich he'd ordered from the cafeteria for lunch. The nurse got me into a sitting position and had me pull my knees up to either side of my chest. I needed assistance as I was not completely in charge of my legs yet. Billy held one leg and the nurse the other. Dr Oscar arrived and put on a facemask and gloves.

'Showtime,' he winked at me.

I pushed until I was red in the face. The epidural had taken the edge off the pain, but had worn off enough for me to have control over the pushing. Between contractions I panted and the nurse mopped my brow.

'You're doing great,' Billy whispered in my ear, kissing my forehead.

'There's the head,' Doctor Oscar announced and Billy dropped my leg to get a better view.

'It looks like a purple walnut,' Billy frowned.

'Do you want a mirror?' asked the nurse, beaming at me.

'Dear God, no,' I answered without hesitation. A powerful sensation tore through my body, impelling me to push until I felt I was turning inside out. A guttural roar from some primal place filled the room and the intense burning between my legs gave way to the slippery sensation that a giant wet fish had slithered from my loins. And then relief. No pain. Nothing.

The moment hung in the air like a freeze frame. Billy's face glowed. I held my breath. Waiting. And then with a frail bleating noise, everything began to move again.

'A son. A beautiful little boy,' Doctor Oscar announced. Billy and I burst into tears as the wet, purple creature was placed on my belly. With tiny hooded grey eyes my little boy blinked at me, trying to focus. Through a curtain of tears I reached out and held his tiny fist. Ben.

Billy leaned in and kissed me, blinking back tears and stroking the slippery pink skin. Our son had a glistening film of fair hair on his head and he licked his lips with the tiniest of tongues. Doctor Oscar helped Billy to cut the umbilical cord. The baby was just perfect.

My life seemed to flash before my eyes and I watched as any need for validation through sex or drugs dissolved into a clear and pure sunrise on a brand-new day. I suddenly understood how deeply my mother must love me. My mother, my self.

All night I held my son, just looking at him sleeping peacefully as the breeze from the warm Darlinghurst night played on our skin. I watched him twitch the corner of his mouth while he slept and I put him to my breast and fed him from my body. We fell into a rhythm as old as time and he squeezed my finger tightly as he sucked.

Billy went out with Jackie and Brian to celebrate.

32.

On Friday, before we left the hospital, I let Billy take Ben for his heel-prick test while I wandered down to the antenatal class. I was still a bit sore and my belly felt like a sack of mashed potato. The Artist was absent again and I was worried.

When the teacher saw me she raised her hand; the whole class turned and, seeing me minus my giant girth, burst into a round of applause. I gave a little self-conscious bow. The teacher came over and took my hand. When I asked if she had seen my friend, she led me out into the corridor.

'Her mother died and she flew back to England. The doctor had to give her permission to fly. She'll be staying there for the birth of her baby.'

This was sad news. I had learned so much from her and from the book she gave me, I wanted to thank her. And I wanted to see my portrait!

Back at home, Billy and I leapt into parenthood with gusto. Billy was a warm and attentive Dad, so proud to have a little boy, and Ben was an easy baby. He fed well and slept well and stayed happy in between. I would drag his little bouncer around the house with me and talk to him while I did the housework.

I began a journal and found that I loved writing in it at the end of each day. *My Mother / My Self* had opened up so many hidden corners of my psyche and I was starting to understand that my adolescent sexual adventures were not at all deviant, but a natural and healthy part of growing up. I had gone on a book-buying spree, discovering a whole new field of literature on the 'self' and on what it meant to be a woman. I realised that I had been acting only semi-consciously for much of my life. Maybe it was becoming a mother, or turning twenty-one, but I felt like I was experiencing a psychological growth spurt. I felt the old fog of shame lifting to make way for a more confident and self-assured version of myself.

I looked in the mirror and saw something in my eyes that I hadn't seen before. I saw my mother looking back at me and I loved her and myself and forgave us both for having drifted apart. I saw that her unhappiness had made me feel that she was unhappy with me. I had made it all about me, as teenagers are wont to do, and adopted the role of the disappointing daughter. But now I understood that her unhappiness was something quite separate from me. I couldn't make her happy. I couldn't make either of my parents proud of me. That had to come from within them. And so I began to let go of my need for their approval, something that had been so fundamentally necessary to me for so long.

It was liberating, as though I had dropped a heavy load that I'd been carrying around behind me. Writing in my journal one night, I addressed the God of my youth: 'You don't have to forgive me, Father, for I have never sinned at all and never will, because sin is something that belongs to you, not to me. I have nothing to confess.' Keeping a journal helped me to make sense of my new thoughts and preserved the new memories I was making. Without it, I felt, my daily life might sink to the bottom of the sea and dissolve.

Filming for *The Clean Machine* was approaching and I was pleased to see my belly shrinking. My breasts, however, had swollen to twice their size, which was extreme for a big-boobed girl.

'They will shrink when you stop feeding, won't they?' Billy asked. He said he'd never seen anything like them, except perhaps in a freak-show porn movie. I had nipples the size of saucers and my bra size was a J. J for juggernauts.

When the first day of filming arrived, I expressed a bottle of milk, left it with Billy and set out for the Botany set. I only had three scenes and we would film them all on the same day. I had been so nervous that morning, I'd considered pulling out. The thought of showing my lactating boobs to Grigor Taylor – not to mention a national television audience – was more than disconcerting.

I arrived on set and met Grigor. He was charming and just as good-looking in person as on TV. Our first scene went well, although my projected measurements were somewhat out and my yellow dress stretched uncomfortably, squashing my breasts into one enormous ball. But I scored my first screen kiss with someone I'd watched on television as a young girl, which was thrilling and a little bit creepy all at the same time.

Next was our bedroom scene. I stripped and slipped into a robe. The set would be a 'closed set', but that still left the actor, director, cameraman, lighting guy and sound guy. When I finally dropped the robe, I couldn't miss the dumbfounded expressions on their faces. I perched on the end of the bed and shook my head, a smile creeping onto my lips. Ken was filming me from behind as promised – but he had me sitting in front of a mirror. Now, that was cheating! But everyone was so business-like, my modesty soon disappeared and I got down to the business of acting. I felt good about my performance and Ken made nice noises about how talented I was. Grigor looked a little pale when I started leaking unexpectedly; as the milk geysers began to spout, I swallowed my pride and asked for a towel.

The show would air a month after editing. I hoped my

performance would redeem me somewhat from the ignominy of *Dead End Drive-In*.

At home, I began thinking about taking little Ben north. Mum was dying to meet him. We had bought a disposable camera and sent her some photos, but she wanted to hold him and play with him. My little brother David was apparently chuffed to be an uncle at such an early age. And I was ready to go home as an adult woman.

33.

We caught the train up to Murwillimbah again when Ben was two months old, this time in a first-class, non-smoking carriage. Between feeds I read more of my self-help books.

'Mumbo jumbo ... new-age gibberish,' Billy said dismissively whenever I tried to share a new insight. I had learned not to react to his criticisms, but they were becoming alarmingly frequent. I was worried about his mood and hoped a stint in the sunshine with the family would do us both good. We could swim and relax and fall back in love.

Home had not changed a bit. The house was still sporting velvet stripes of wallpaper, bad shag-pile carpet and a vinyl and bamboo bar. The children had grown some. Mum was looking more tired and pained and the atmosphere between her and Dad was still strained. Annie had fallen in love, finished school and blossomed into a beautiful young woman. She was living in Southport with her boyfriend now and they seemed like a nice couple. Mum and Dad were of course not happy about it, but they'd become more relaxed about letting their children make their own decisions. Perhaps my shocking departure had cleared the path a little for my younger siblings.

Ben was an instant hit.

'Let's get him baptised while you're here,' Mum suggested with a sudden rush of excitement.

Billy and I looked at one another. I inhaled sharply while he gave a smirk.

'I'm an atheist,' he said. 'But it's your call, Nik. You're the Catholic.'

I looked at Mum, her green eyes staring up at me hopefully. To my mind it was ridiculous to think that a sprinkle of water and a few words could mean the difference between life everlasting and eternal damnation. What sort of God would do that to a little child? But Mum believed. Perhaps that was her grand passion. She was afraid for Ben's soul and I remembered that she had described sprinkling holy water on each of our heads in the labour ward, just in case misfortune struck before the official christening. This mattered to her.

'That's a lovely idea, Mum.' It was the very least I could do for her.

She beamed a radiant smile and touched little Ben on the head.

'Billy and I want to go to the beach for a dip,' I said to Mum. 'Would you look after Benny for an hour?'

'Oh, yes, please.' The new grandmother was in her element.

I pulled out the black swimsuit that had brought me such pain during the Coke audition and threw on a sarong. Billy and I walked up Monaco Street, over the three bridges to the sand. New homes had been built where old fibro shacks once stood. The skyline of Surfers had gone ballistic. We passed two metermaids on their way to Surfers, tottering on sequined stilettos, their tanned skin glistening beneath gold bikinis. Instead of being appalled, I smiled at them. They would have been perfect in a Coke commercial.

We strolled along the beach, our feet digging into the sand like a mountaineer's pickaxes. The water was sapphire blue and a handful of clouds sailed gently on the breeze while seagulls fought and squawked with malicious mirth. Pippies and shells speckled the foamy waterline, tumbling as the froth ebbed and flowed. I drew a deep breath, filled my nostrils with the briny air and threw off the sarong.

The water was like taking a cold bath in Alka-seltzer. The sting of salt in my eyes and the taste of the ocean made me feel at home. I was still the little girl who'd splashed naked in the shallows when the Gold Coast was a sleepy seaside village. I dove beneath a rolling wave and felt the powerful surge above me. I remembered making sandcastles with my mother, collecting shells and decorating our creations. She was so beautiful with her golden tan and wide smile. We were so alike in many ways and I was proud of that. We were also very different and that too was okay.

I broke the surface and looked back to shore. Billy was riding a wave and laughing loudly at the rush. Behind the wall of high-rises I saw the voluptuous green lines of the hinterland, lying like a sleeping Amazon behind the glitter. She was beautiful.

I began to realise that I couldn't hate the Gold Coast anymore. My rejection of her had been a case of self-loathing, for in many ways I was the embodiment of the Gold Coast. We both wore masks but there was substance beneath the tinsel. Now, in the tumultuous surf, I felt her power. 'You can't take this away from me,' she murmured from the water. This, the sea, was her soul and it was as pure as the smile on my baby's face.

As I tasted the tang of salt on my lips and let the water caress me, I cried long overdue tears. I no longer had to be the person I was expected to be, but I didn't need to rebel against that either. I spat a mouthful of cold ocean through my gapped teeth, up toward the sun, and felt the warmth on my face. I was me. Flawed, perverse, egotistical, afraid, beautiful, passionate – just me.

My grand passion was still winning an Oscar and it would happen when it happened – or I would die grateful just for having reached for that star. The bumper sticker had been right: passion was grand. But it could have said more: 'You must have one grand passion, but two or three would be better.' I had a new passion for love. Love for myself and love for those that mattered to me. Billy mattered. My parents mattered. Ben mattered. And I mattered; I was my own work of art. There were highlights, shadows and brushstrokes that had been added by the people in my life, all of them. And they made my portrait all the richer.

After bathing Ben and powdering his soft, doughy skin, Mum showed me into Annie's former bedroom, where a hired cot was pressed against the wall. In it sat Andy Gibb, large as life, grinning moronically.

'He's so bright and colourful,' Mum said. 'It'll give the little man something to look at.'

I laughed and placed Ben at the other end of the mattress. His little eyes tracked straight to the oversized rabbit.

'Gee, you used to love that rabbit,' Mum said with a nostalgic sigh.

'Oh, Mum,' I laughed. 'You have no idea!'

EPILOGUE
Autumn, 1988

The perfume of petrol fumes wafted up to our apartment from Old South Head Road and the autumn breeze flirted with the curtains. The television was turned up loud as *The Factory* pumped out its Saturday morning smorgasbord of music videos, interviews and comedy sketches.

'It's coming up next!' I shouted to Billy, who appeared with a ham, cheese and tomato toastie and a weak cup of milky coffee.

'Thanks.'

I sipped at the coffee but I was too excited to do more than pick at the crusts of the toast.

Ben was padding about the living room, his chubby little legs poking stiffly from either side of his nappy and a two-toothed grin revealing his pride in being newly bipedal.

Alex Papps, host of *The Factory* and a *Home and Away* heart-throb, appeared on screen, ready to introduce his next guest.

'Look! It's Joy!' I screamed, jumping to my feet and sending bits of molten ham and cheese flying onto the couch. There next to Alex, my mate Joy Smithers was grinning her pretty dimpled grin. Her short blonde hair was spiked and she was looking very rock and roll. She and Alex shot the breeze for a while, discussing Joy's latest role in the ABC series *Stringer*, which featured Joy as the lead singer of an all-girl rock group. I played the bass player. I was smiling so hard my cheeks were splitting.

'It's coming up. It's coming up! Have you got the tape in?'

Billy fiddled with the video player and gave me the thumbs up. 'Good to go.'

'Well, press it now. Press it now! I want all of this, too.' I was jabbering like a mad woman.

With perfect timing, Billy hit 'record' just as Alex introduced a preview clip from the series.

'It's me!' I hooted. 'Look, Benny. Mummy's on TV.'

We all stared at the screen as Joy and I, in character, discussed the finer points of post-feminism with a male character. My hair was impressive. It was teased into an unruly bush on top of my head, with straggles of red hanging over my one exposed shoulder. I looked gaunt but good. Dark eyes and nonchalant attitude. We'd filmed the scene well after midnight and a few cans of beer.

Ben waddled to the television and touched my face, then frowned confusedly back at me.

'Out of the way, honey,' I said, scooping him into my arms.

Back to Joy and Alex. Joy introduced the film-clip for her single 'Young Love', which featured *Stringer*'s all-girl band. Then the clip came on and I danced along with Ben, while Billy started laughing.

'Look at you; you look quite the rock star.'

Man, I was swinging that bass around like I was born to rock. The camera zoomed in and caught me singing sideways into the microphone, doing back-ups to Joy's lovely voice. I shook my tresses and gave a Chrissy Amphlett pout. All those years of watching rock stars shake their thing had paid off. I was gyrating and banging that fret board like a true pro.

'Your fingers give you away,' Billy smiled, shaking his head.

'Yeah, well, only a real bass player could tell,' I snapped.

I had tried to learn the bass line so that I would look like a real bass player, but the truth was, I was only miming. In fact, I wasn't singing, either, but it didn't matter to me. It looked real enough. And I knew I'd probably never, ever be on TV as a rock star again.

Stringer was the most fun I'd had as an actress. Playing a member of an all-girl band had let me act out my childhood fantasies.

'That was unreal!' Billy cheered as the clip finished and an ad break hit the screen.

'It was, wasn't it? Completely unreal,' I smiled.

Ben and I replayed the video over and over for the rest of the day, in between phone calls from friends who'd witnessed my moment of glory. It wasn't going to win me an Academy Award, but it felt absolutely fantastic.

I was a rock star. Even if I was only pretending.

POSTSCRIPT

Billy and I moved back to the Gold Coast, got married and had another beautiful son, Toby. We separated and divorced two years later. Billy has remarried and I thank him for the love we shared and the children we created. Both our sons grew up to be rock musicians.

Rhonda is a successful optometrist, lives in London and still likes going to rock and roll gigs.

Jackie was murdered on the Gold Coast in the early nineties.

Bob was inducted into the ARIA Hall of Fame.

Mum and Dad separated not long after Toby was born but have remained friends. Our family has stayed strong and close and my siblings are my best friends.

I live with my husband, Zeus, and three youngest children, Harry, Mia and Tom, in the Gold Coast hinterland with a view of the high-rise sprawl. At night the lights are beautiful and I am thankful for having grown up where I did.

I do not yet have an Oscar but I still believe in the dream. I have not yet strolled the sidewalks of New York but I hope that when I do, I find a portrait of my naked pregnant form, for that marked the day I began to see with my own eyes.

ACKNOWLEDGEMENTS

With gratitude to ...

The judging panel of the Queensland Premier's Literary Awards for shortlisting my manuscript; my super-agent, Sophie Hamley, for her confidence and support; my publisher, Chris Feik, for his belief in the book; and my editor, Denise O'Dea, for being so gentle with a first-timer. Her guiding hand has polished this little tale into something I am very proud of.

Thanks to Gemma Ward for her laughter and love and for being my first reader.

This book is made up of a cast of interesting characters and I wouldn't be who I am today without them. I am grateful to still have so many of you in my life (thank you, Facebook) and often miss those who only briefly flitted by.

Great dollops of love to my incredible and unique children, Ben, Toby, Harrison Black, Mia and Tom. This book of mine is no excuse for bad behaviour, so don't ever try it on. Just because I did it, doesn't make it right!

Much love and thanks to the family – Mum, Dad, Annie, Rachel and David – for all that you are. What a great heritage.

But most of all I thank my husband, Zeus – my rock and my champion. He suggested I write this story and I'm so glad that I did.

www.ingramcontent.com/pod-product-compliance
Lightning Source LLC
Chambersburg PA
CBHW071154160426
43196CB00011B/2078